the
ACCURATE
TABLE SAW

the
ACCURATE
TABLE SAW

SIMPLE JIGS AND SAFE SETUPS

Ian Kirby

CAMbIUM PRESS
Newtown

The Accurate Table Saw

©1998 by Ian Kirby

ISBN 0-9643999-5-4

First printing: April 1998
Second printing: April 2000
Printed in the United States of America

Published by
    Cambium Press
    PO Box 909
    Bethel, CT 06801
        tel 203-778-2782 fax 203-778-2785
        email TABLESAW@CAMBIUMPRESS.COM

Distributed to the book trade by
    Independent Publishers Group
    814 N. Franklin St.
    Chicago, IL 60610
        tel 800-888-4741 fax 312-337-5985

**Library of Congress
Cataloging-in-Publication Data**
Kirby, Ian J., 1932-
    The accurate table saw : simple jigs and safe setups / Ian J. Kirby.
        p.   cm.
    Includes index.
    ISBN 0-9643999-5-4
    1. Circular saws.   I. Title
TT186.K574   1998
621.9'3--dc21   98-18087
                                        CIP

CONTENTS

Preface

To use a table saw safely and accurately you need to understand two things.

How to set up the saw.

How to operate the saw for each kind of cut.

Both of these are complex, though complex doesn't mean difficult or hard to understand. Complex means there are a number of things involved in each process, and you have to get all of them right.

The past few decades have seen a great resurgence in woodworking by the amateur and small shop professional. This has created a competitive marketplace for tools and machines. You can buy a low-price bench-top saw that will do the same four basic operations as an industrial machine costing 50 times as much. The difference is size, plus the industrial machine is a turn-key tool. It's ready to go, while the low-price model isn't. The good news is that whichever machine you own, the knowledge you need to operate it is practically the same.

Ian Kirby, Milford, CT USA, April 1998

Danger and your table saw

by Les Winter, PE and Neal A. Growney, PE, Forensic Engineers

Woodworking machinery is fast, powerful, and capable of causing serious injury. As in many other endeavors, small-shop and amateur practitioners look to the commercial world for guidance regarding safety. We expect them to set a good example. For woodworkers this is a mistake, because in this regard, industrial woodworking shops are among the most backward workplaces in modern industry.

The table saw came into use around 1800, and blade guards were patented as early as 1871. Yet even today, simple protection schemes, long accepted in the metalworking trades, are shunned by the woodworking trade.

The U.S. Consumer Product Safety Commission estimates that from 1974 through 1995 there were 418,408 bench saw or table saw accidents nationwide, with 29,824 in 1995 alone. When the magazine *Fine Woodworking* surveyed its readers, it found that one-third of the accidents cost fingers. This implies about 9900 finger amputations in 1995. Looking forward, we can anticipate another 10,000 saw amputations every year. The good news is, you don't have to be among them.

The essence of danger

Injuries arise from danger. Danger has two components:

hazard,

exposure.

A **hazard** has the potential to cause injury: a razor blade qualifies as a hazard because it can cut you. However, a naked razor blade on the moon poses no threat and is not dangerous. The same blade in your trouser pocket is another matter. The difference is exposure. **Exposure** is the likelihood of coming into contact with the hazard. It is the combination of hazard and exposure that makes something dangerous.

Reducing the exposure makes a hazardous condition less dangerous. Less exposure means less danger; more exposure means more danger. Note that this calculation does not include any factor for experience or carefulness, because neither of these reduces the danger level. The level of danger results solely from hazard and exposure.

Responses to danger

Good machinery designers recognize the hazard and then:

try to design the hazard out,

guard to reduce the exposure,

warn the operator.

Clearly, the design fix is infinitely superior to guarding and warning. Guarding, which means a system that includes top guard plus splitter and antikickback devices, is better than warning. Warning alone, like experience and carefulness, doesn't reduce danger. However, guarding and warning together may be the best we can do.

On the table saw, the unguarded spinning blade is what offers the two components of danger: it is hazardous, and it is exposed. We can't design out the hazard, without inventing some new way of cutting wood. We can only guard the blade, and warn the operator. A useful warning is:

DANGER.
DO NOT OPERATE WITHOUT GUARDS IN PLACE.

Many table saw operators pervert this type of warning. They acknowledge the danger, resolve to be careful, and then work with an unguarded blade. This approach does not work, for three reasons:

1. Resolving to take care is not the same as studying and practicing to acquire knowledge and skill.

2. Even with knowledge and skill, humans are neither perfect nor entirely predictable.

3. Materials are not perfect and their imperfections may not be visible at the outset.

We are not capable of avoiding mistakes. We can't maintain concentration over time. We can't predict how a particular board will react when sawn. If we introduce an unguarded spinning blade into this imperfect environment, we guarantee that injuries will occur. The only question is when.

Seat belts and smoke detectors

We regularly deal with hazards in our daily lives. We install smoke detectors and purchase fire insurance even though we don't expect fires. We wear seat belts even though we don't expect to crash, and we buy health insurance even though we don't expect, on any given day, to be taken ill. We take a sober look at reality and, even in the face of low probability of occurrence, we take precautions "just in case."

Why do woodworkers suspend this ordinary level of judgment at the workshop door? Why do we not insist upon guarding the table saw? Here is the simple answer:

The guards that originally came with our table saws do not work very well. In many applications they make it awkward to work and slow us down. Poor guards train woodworkers not to work safely. Accordingly, we remove the guards and take our chances. Instead of having the insurance that the guard was intended to provide, we settle for being careful.

Even if being careful was an effective accident deterrent for woodworkers (and it most assuredly is not), others who visit our shops (wives, children, friends) are exposed to the saw's hazards. A kicked-back piece of wood might miss the sawyer and strike the visitor. The visitor may place her hand on the saw without realizing that it is running. So the hazard we expose threatens not only ourselves but our visitors as well.

What to do about safety

Blade exposed for photographic clarity.

There are three steps you can take to immediately reduce your level of danger around the table saw.

1. Stop saying "remove the guard" and start being accurate about it. Say, "Expose the blade." (Doesn't this sound odd: "Blade exposed for photographic clarity"?) If we accept that exposing a spinning blade creates danger, then we must find ways to guard it in order to reduce the danger and still do our work efficiently.

2. If the top guard, splitter and antikickback pawls that you own will not permit you to work efficiently and safely, buy or make better ones. This book will show you some of the alternatives.

3. If your guard system will not permit you to make some cut, and you can't obtain or devise a guard that will work, then you are using the wrong tool for that job. Get the correct tool, because the table saw is not it.

Will woodworkers ever get to the point of absolute safety? **Every injury is a sequence of events like the links of a chain. Break one link, and the chain is broken.**

You can avoid injuries by planning what you are going to do, by setting up correctly, and by taking reasonable care. Using a guard system is part of planning and setup. A properly guarded saw, used with reasonable care, is highly unlikely to cause serious injury.

Despite what you may have experienced in the past, it's almost always possible to find a way to guard the blade and to work efficiently and safely.

So far we have talked about the nature of danger, guarding theory, and the possibility of preventing "blade-contact" accidents. Aside from dust collection, which itself requires a book to explain, there remain two main hazards in table saw work. These are electrical shock and kickback.

Don't be shocked

Modern table saws come equipped with grounding-type three-prong plugs. The ground prong connects the metal chassis of the saw to the earth. A grounded tool cannot become electrified and shock you. If you have a modern saw with a grounding-type plug, make certain that it is not altered and that it is plugged into a grounding-type receptacle. Damp basements and old tools with failing insulation are a dangerous combination. If you have an older saw and are in doubt about its grounding, do not hesitate. Consult any licensed electrician.

Kickback

"Kickback" is when the wood or pieces of it are thrown back at the sawyer. Understanding kickback is not intuitive and its causes are not obvious. The danger is downplayed by TV and woodworking video stars, trade-show demonstrators and professional tradespeople who regularly work without kickback protection devices. The injuries that can be caused, however, are serious and can be fatal.

Without appropriate guards, there is no question as to whether kickback will happen. It will. The question is whether it will happen in a manner that produces an injury. Will it be too weak to hurt us? Or, will the kickback be stopped before the accident occurs?

Kicked-back wood is propelled by the rotating blade. Typical 10-inch table saw blades rotate at 4,000 RPM. This is a tooth-speed of almost 120 MPH. A chunk of wood caught by a tooth of a 10-inch blade can be released at that speed and fired straight back at the sawyer. How does this work?

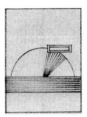

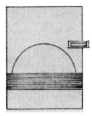

Unplug your table saw, expose the blade and raise it to its maximum height. Attach a clothespin to the rear-most tooth, the one closest to the table surface, and stand the pin upright. Now rotate the blade slowly in the normal cutting direction. The clothespin first rises vertically and then, following the arc of the blade, moves forward. At the top of its travel, the clothespin will be moving horizontally toward the operator. If the blade were moving at speed, and the clothespin broke free just at top dead center, the pin would be thrown forward at the tip speed of 120 MPH. This is exactly how a major league pitcher accelerates an overarm fastball. A sawyer experiencing kickback is looking at a piece of wood coming at him even faster than that fastball. There is no time to duck out of the way.

Kickback will occur if the wood distorts so the sawn kerf closes and pinches the rear blade teeth, just like our clothespin. If the wood grabs tight, the blade will lift it from the table and kick it back at the sawyer. Another way to cause kickback is to crowd the wood sideways into the rear of the blade. This also occurs if a small piece of scrap rotates and jams between the rip fence and the side or the rear of the blade. Similarly, a piece that falls into the table insert slot at the back of the blade can be picked up by a rising rear tooth. In each case, the wood is in tight contact with a rear tooth, it rises above the table with that tooth, then it's pitched forward at the top of the tooth's arc.

How can this danger be avoided? First, the rip fence must not crowd the wood to the back of the blade. Second, we must deny the wood access to the rear of the blade by using the splitter (also called a spreader or riving knife). Third, to prevent wood from moving forward toward the sawyer, we must use anti-kickback pawls and we must keep them sharp. Fourth, we must prevent small scrap from being wedged against the blade by the rip fence. And finally, we must guard the blade.

10,000 fingers

So there you have the major table saw hazards. Thousands of amputations occur each year because woodworkers work with improperly guarded machines. Here's one way you can break one link in the injury-causing chain: Use a guard system.

The table saw, correctly set up, can cut within .01 inch of the mark.

CHAPTER 1

What Is Accuracy?

"Accuracy" is relative. It depends on the material, on the measuring tools, and on the objective. Accuracy in soft materials like leather is not the same as accuracy in wood, and accuracy in hard materials like metal is different again.

Woodworkers are concerned with three different kinds of accuracy:

dimensional accuracy

angular accuracy

surface regularity.

When you are sawing wood, accuracy depends on a chain of events involving the flatness of the saw table, the setup of the saw, the precision of the saw blade, and the unpredictable nature of the material itself. Depending on what you are making, acceptable accuracy in wood varies across three full orders of magnitude, from +/-1inch to .001 inch. In many situations, what is acceptable is what looks accurate, whether or not it actually is.

Dimensional accuracy varies by about one order of magnitude, from 1/8 inch or 1/10 inch to 1/64 inch or 1/100 inch. If you are building a house, cutting a 2x4 to within 1/8 inch of the specified measurement is close enough. If you are making a fine piece of furniture, +/- 1/8 inch is far too crude a measurement, but a tolerance of +/- .01 inch is close enough. More to the point, that's about the limit of accuracy you can achieve with ordinary woodworking tools, in a material as variable as wood. In most woodworking, making parts that are all the same size, or that will fit a given space like a drawer front in its opening, is more important than precisely specified dimensions.

Angular accuracy normally is not a matter of plus or minus. It's either square or it isn't. However, if you were to measure angular accuracy with sophisticated instruments, you would find that normal woodworking accuracy is within a minute of arc, that is, 1/60 of a degree.

Surface regularity has three aspects: flatness, smoothness, and twist. The first two can be grossly checked with a straight edge. It will reveal deviations from flat of about .01 inch. However, a smoothing plane can take a shaving that is less than .001 inch in thickness, and your fingertips can detect the difference. So, while it is difficult to measure surface smoothness, it is easy to assess it by touch, and tolerances of +/- .001 are commonly achieved in wood. Nevertheless, a surface can be apparently flat and perfectly smooth and still twist like a potato chip.

Measure the wood, not the saw

A table saw is a breakdown tool, not a finishing tool. It does not produce a finished surface. Nevertheless, when it is set up right with a carbide-tipped saw blade, it can saw pieces of wood that are the same size and shape.

To check the saw's performance, observe and measure the wood, not the tool. This is not to say that your set-up can be inaccurate, nor that you don't need measuring tools to tune and adjust your saw, because you do. But the saw set-up is only as accurate as the results, and an accurately sawn workpiece is what matters.

Measuring tools

No matter what saw you own, if you are striving for accuracy you need measuring and marking tools. You must have all of these tools in order to set up your saw and check the accuracy of the workpiece — there are no shortcuts. These measuring tools are not specific to the table saw. You can use them to assess the condition of any machine, and the results of any woodworking operation.

The kit of measuring tools used in this book includes:

Straight edge, 24-inch. Assesses flatness.

Pair of **winding sticks**, 20-inch. Measures twist.

Square with **graduated rule**, 12-inch. Verifies 90 degrees.

Dial caliper, 6-inch. Measures small distances.

Metal **tape measure**, 1 inch x 25 feet. Measures large distances.

Protractor and **sliding bevel**. Measures angles.

Hand lens, 4x magnification. Helps you see.

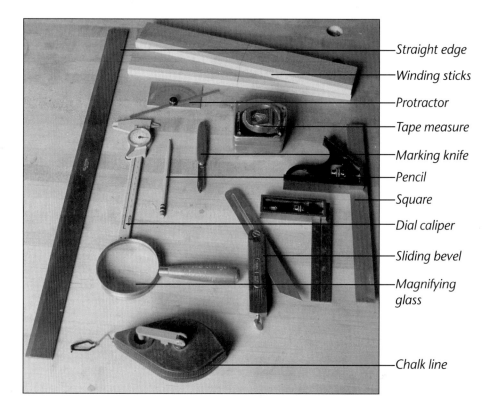

— Straight edge
— Winding sticks
— Protractor
— Tape measure
— Marking knife
— Pencil
— Square
— Dial caliper
— Sliding bevel
— Magnifying glass
— Chalk line

Checking dimensional accuracy

Dimensional accuracy means you want to be able to cut pieces of wood to the same known size, over and over again. It's not a matter of sawing just one piece to the right size, it's sawing them all to the same right size. While the right size maybe a given dimension, woodworkers more often work to a fit: the pieces fit the space, the joint shoulders are the same distance apart, even if they are not exactly the specified distance.

There are two ways to check dimensional accuracy.

Measure the wood, using a ruler, tape measure or dial caliper. Your choice of instrument depends on the span in question.

Directly observe the wood. Saw two pieces of wood to the same settings and fit them together. Orient both face sides the same way, one piece on top of the other. You will be able to see, and feel, whether or not they are the same size. Your fingertips can detect size differences of less than .001 inch.

Once the saw is correctly set up, dimensional accuracy results mainly from operator consistency. When ripping, this means the workpiece has to have a face edge, you have to hold this edge against the fence with consistent firmness, and you must push it with consistent force throughout. When cross-cutting, the face edge has to contact the crosscut fence tightly and firmly, and it has to bear on the stop-block with consistent pressure. In either case, the operator has to make sure there are no waste chips interfering with how the workpiece beds on the table and bears against the fence.

Measure the wood, not the saw, to assess whether the machine is cutting accurately.

The fingertips assess whether these two pieces of wood were sawn to the same size.

Dial caliper

A dial caliper measures distances to a high degree of accuracy. It can make inside measurements as well as outside ones, so it can measure the thickness of the workpiece, or the width of a groove.

You can buy machinist's calipers that will measure .0001 of an inch, but that is more accuracy than most woodworkers will ever need. While you could spend a lot of money for a machinist's caliper with a digital readout, there are two affordable alternatives. Most hardware stores sell a gray plastic caliper with a green dial. It measures 64ths and 100ths of an inch. The plastic is sturdy enough to withstand being knocked around the shop, and if it does get chewed up, the replacement cost is not high. Most metalworking suppliers sell imported and affordable dial calipers that measure to .001 inch.

To use a caliper, plant the fixed jaw on the workpiece and press it there with your finger. Then bring the movable jaw into contact with the wood. Be sure the caliper is sitting squarely on the wood, and isn't cocked to either side.

Most woodworkers don't have a dial caliper, but once you add one to your tool kit you will wonder how you ever got along without it.

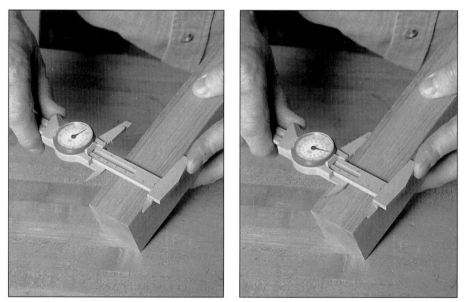

Plant the fixed jaw of the dial caliper on the workpiece, then bring the movable jaw into contact.

Tape measure

A 25-foot steel tape is always close to hand for most woodworkers. Although it can measure all distances up to the length of the tape, the steel rule and dial caliper are more accurate over small distances.

If you check one tape against another, you'll be surprised by how much they vary. It usually doesn't matter, as long as you use the same tape throughout a job.

One subtlety of the steel tape is the hook that keeps it from retracting into its case. The hook is always loose on its rivets, and it's supposed to be that way. The amount of looseness corresponds to the thickness of the hook itself, which makes the tape accurate for inside measure as well as for outside measure. This lets you use the tape to measure the distance between the saw fence and the blade.

Checking angular accuracy

"Angular accuracy," most of the time, means square, 90 degrees, precisely. It's either square, or it isn't.

Use the square to check the newly sawn edge in two places, a couple of inches in from either end of the board. There are only three possible conditions:

It's square at both ends. You can assume it's also square all along the length.

It's not square, but the deviation is about the same at either end. The saw blade was not square to the table, so correct it and cut the wood again.

It's not square, but the deviation shifts from one side of the wood to the other — the sawn edge twists. The most likely cause is that the face of the wood is not flat, so check it with your winding sticks. It's possible that a small particle was trapped, holding one corner up off the saw table. Perhaps the wood's face side was up instead of down on the table. While it's tempting to declare that the saw table itself must be in twist, it's more likely to be poor operator procedure.

Square

You can buy a fixed-blade square, or a combination square, which has a moveable, graduated blade. The blade can be removed and used as a rule for measuring distances up to its own length, which can be 6, 12, 18 or 24 inches.

Quality makes a real difference. Buy an accurately made machinist's square, not a crude imitation — good brands are Starrett in the US, and Moore & Wright in the UK. One way to tell the difference at a glance is by looking at the graduations incised into the metal rule, or blade. They should be fine and precise, not crude, paint-filled stampings.

To use the combination square to assess a piece of wood, slide the stock toward the center of the rule and tighten the thumbscrerw. Place the stock firmly against the face or edge of the wood, then lower it until the rule makes contact. Don't slide it like a trombone, because you can't get an accurate reading.

When you hold the wood against the square, you're looking for any deviation. Unlike our tools for measuring dimensions, which tell you exactly how big the wood is, the square doesn't produce an angular measurement other than 90 degrees. It's either square, or it isn't.

Dropping and banging around may raise a burr on one corner of the square. You'll feel it as you lower the stock onto the workpiece. Remove the burr on 400-grit carborundum paper held flat on a sheet of glass.

Press the stock of the square against the wood, then lower the blade onto it. Look toward the light and you'll see any deviation from 90 degrees.

Sliding bevel and protractor

The sliding bevel is the traditional tool for managing angles other than 90 degrees. While it does not measure an angle, it allows you to transfer one from drawing to workpiece or miter gauge, or from workpiece to workpiece.

In order to measure angles, you have to borrow another tool from the machinist's kit, the protractor.

It's often difficult to directly measure an angle on the wood itself. Instead, take the angle with the sliding bevel and transfer it to the bench top or to a piece of paper. Then measure the drawing with the protractor.

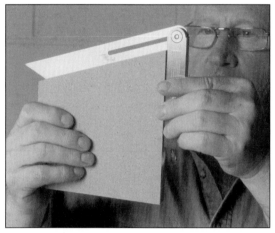

To measure an angle, take it off the wood with the sliding bevel.

Transfer the angle to the edge of a board.

Measure the transferred angle with the machinist's protractor, left, or with a plastic school protractor, below.

Checking surface regularity

The third aspect of accuracy is surface regularity. You can assess flatness with a straight edge and winding sticks. To assess smoothness, however, the only tools woodworkers have are the eye and hand.

While the table saw does not leave wood ready for finishing, it is able to create a flat and smooth surface without deep score marks, gouges or scratches. While a sawn surface won't be smooth enough for varnishing, it should be smooth enough to glue.

The 4x magnifying glass can tell you how your tools are performing. The marks left by the saw blade are an important diagnostic tool. They are the clue to knowing whether you are feeding the wood correctly, whether you have set the fence correctly, and whether the blade is damaged.

Straight edge

A straight edge assesses straightness. It doesn't do anything else. It's not a rulcr or a yardstick. It is a precision instrument, a good one is expensive, but it really is essential. The 24-inch size is good for general woodworking and machine tune-up. It will be accurate to within .0005 inch.

When you are doing accurate work, the straight edge has to be close at hand. Since its value depends totally on its accurate edge, you must take care to keep from damaging it. When you're using the straight edge to check the flatness of a surface, set it gently on the work. Don't bang it around. Lay it flat on the bench, not balanced on other stuff.

Reserve the beveled side of the straight edge for checking straightness of surfaces. Use its back edge as a guide for trimming leather or veneers. Keep it clean and bright.

The straight edge tells you whether the wood is straight.

Winding sticks

Winding sticks measure twist. They come in pairs and they are usually shop made.

The important requirement of a winding stick is that its long edges be parallel. Make yourself a couple of pairs, one about 14 inches long and one a short 6 inches. There should be a mark at the center of each stick. Shop-made sticks often have the top edge of inlaid ebony or holly, for easy visibility.

Winding sticks are easy to use. Place each stick across the workpiece near the ends, parallel to one another, then sight their top edges. Crouch down to do this, line up the center marks on the two sticks, and keep your head straight. You'll be able to see whether the sticks are parallel, and if not, how much the surface twists.

Check flat from one end to the other, but also check from the middle of the workpiece to either end. It's possible for the ends to be true while something strange occurs in between. Use the sticks the same way on the edge of the workpiece.

To assess twist, set the winding sticks on the face or edge of the wood, align the center marks, and sight from one to the other.

Make winding sticks of dry, quarter-sawn hardwood. The edges must be straight and parallel.

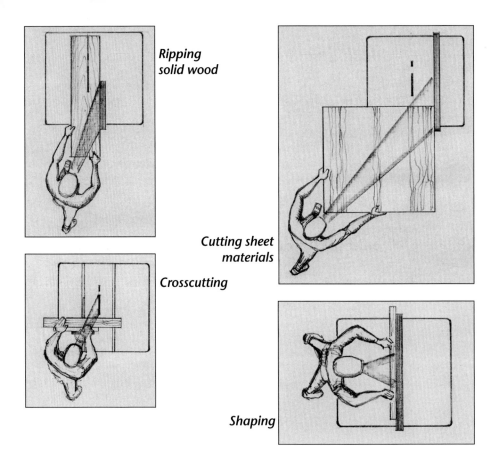

Ripping
solid wood

Cutting sheet
materials

Crosscutting

Shaping

CHAPTER 2

Choosing a Saw

Saws are designated by blade size. The 10-inch blade is standard for the home shop and small professional shop, although some bench-top models have 8-inch blades. There are three basic types of 10-inch table saw:

Bench-top saws,

Contractor saws,

Cabinet saws.

Which saw you choose depends on several factors that only you can evaluate. They are:

How much money do you wish to spend?

How much woodworking do you do?

What kind of woodworking do you do?

How much space do you have?

A table saw does four things

A table saw does four things. It can:

rip solid wood,

cut sheet materials,

crosscut,

shape.

By way of basic definitions, when ripping, crosscutting, or when sawing sheet materials, the saw cuts the material into two pieces. The piece you want is called the **workpiece**. The other piece is called the **falling board**. It's not "waste" or "scrap," because it frequently is larger than the workpiece and will be further divided into another workpiece with another falling board. **Sheet materials** are mentioned throughout this book — they come as 4x8 sheets or panels, and the term embraces plywood, particleboard, and medium-density fiberboard or MDF, wall paneling and siding, and high-density fiberboard (Masonite).

When the saw does not divide the workpiece into two pieces, the operation is called **shaping**. Shaping includes sawing a groove, profiling the edge with a rebate or a molding, and most joint-making operations. You can shape the wood with the saw blade, with a dado head, or with a molding head and special molding cutters.

Whenever you offer a piece of wood to the table saw, it must have a flat face to sit on the table, and it must have one straight edge to run against the fence. The flat face is called the **face side** and the straight edge is called the **face edge**.

The face side and face edge are **reference surfaces**. Whether you are working by hand or with machines or both, understanding the importance of the face side and edge is vital throughout the whole process of construction (page 64).

The faces and edges on wood as it comes from the lumberyard usually are neither flat nor square. If the wood doesn't have a face side and a face edge, it can not be cut to accurate dimensions on the table saw. It can only be rough-cut oversize, or else cut more or less inaccurately. In order to do accurate work, you will need to use the table saw along with other tools to prepare the wood with a face side and edge.

Bench-top saw

Bench-top saws combine the saw motor and blade arbor in a single direct-drive mechanism. They commonly take 8-inch blades, though some manufacturers now offer 10-inch models. These saws are low in price and don't take much space, and consequently they outsell the other styles by about three to one.

Although bench-top saws come with a small table, they can be built into the center of a larger system. However, an 8-inch blade limits how high you can raise the blade above the table. The direct drive also limits the power that can be delivered to the blade, and the amount of cutting you can do before the motor overheats.

After-market fences and guards are not readily available for all makes of bench-top saws. This makes it difficult to improve the basic package that comes from the manufacturer. Nevertheless, if you have one of these saws, or decide to buy one, all the subsequent discussion in this book applies. You will need to pay close attention to setup and operator proce- dures, and if you do, you will be able to produce accurate and safe work.

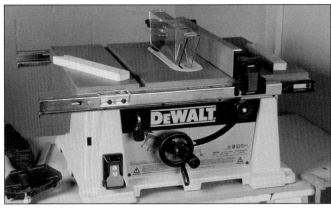

10-inch DeWalt bench-top saw has been re-engineered with a rack-and-pinion fence and a splitter that rises and falls. It has a range of accessories and aftermarket parts.

10-inch Sears Craftsman is a low-priced bench-top saw that comes with a sheet metal stand.

Contractor's saw

Contractor-type saws use a belt drive from the motor to the blade arbor. They have the motor hanging off the back side of the mechanism, so its weight tensions the drive belt. This allows the machine to accept motors of varying size and power, and the blade to be raised without interference from the motor. Although these saws have a tilting arbor, the design of the mechanism means the tilt mechanism can't be accurate (page 30).

Contractor saws typically come with a 20-inch by 27-inch table. Manufacturers offer various styles of cast-iron and sheet-metal table extension, or you can build your own out of wood.

This style of saw was developed during the housing boom that followed the Second World War. It was relatively cheap, portable, and accurate enough for job-site carpentry. Since then, thousands of contractor's saws have found their way into home shops and small professional shops. They're generally regarded as the basic saw for any kind of serious work.

Because contractor's saws are so popular, manufacturers have devised a large number of aftermarket fences, guards and other accessories. These make it possible to improve the basic saw, and to extend its capabilities.

Delta 10-inch contractor's saw has a cast-iron wing to the left of the blade, and a particleboard extension to the right.

Cabinet saw

Cabinet saws not only separate the motor from the drive mechanism, they also have a good arbor-tilting mechanism. This makes it possible to engineer accuracy into the mechanism. For this reason, cabinet saws are generally considered necessary in all but the smallest professional shops.

Cabinet saws come with blades ranging from 10 inches up to 16 inches, and with motors up to 5 HP. They can run all day without overheating, and can manage virtually any size of wood. Most of the aftermarket fences and guards you would have to purchase for smaller saws come as standard equipment. There's little need to improve the package that comes from the manufacturer, though there is a large inventory of aftermarket equipment available.

A cabinet saw is at the heart of this busy professional shop.

Chop saw

This is a book about table saws and it doesn't do to wander off topic, but if you are equipping a shop for the first time, there is an addition you ought to consider. The advent of the sliding-arm chop saw has resulted in a stunningly accurate tool for crosscutting solid wood. These saws will cut 3 inches deep on a 12-inch width. You can see what you are doing, and you can sneak up on the cut in increments as fine as .01 inch.

What the chop saw can't do is rip solid wood, or break down sheets of plywood. Many woodworkers therefore make space for a chop saw and a table saw. Use the chop saw for crosscutting and the table saw for ripping, and you'll get the best out of each machine.

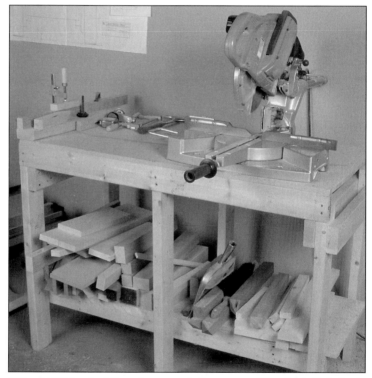

Hitachi 10-inch sliding chop saw is the crosscutting tool of choice in this small shop. Blocks at left support long stock.

Contractor's saw has aftermarket fence, splitter, guard, and extension tables; with shop-made rear table extension, miter-gauge fence, and push sticks. The aftermarket accessories cost almost as much as the saw itself.

CHAPTER 3

Setting Up Your Saw

The care with which you set up your saw has a lot to do with how accurately it can work for you. While some owner's manuals show good setup procedures, others hover between incomprehensible and nonexistent. Throughout the setup, your priority should be to understand how the mechanisms work and what their limitations are. This will equip you to eliminate slop and ambiguity, and achieve accuracy.

The saw has three **controls:**
on-off switch
blade elevation handwheel
arbor tilt handwheel

The saw comes with three standard **accessories**, each requiring alignment:
fence
table insert
miter gauge

The saw comes with three pieces of **safety apparatus.**
splitter
blade guard
antikickback pawls

There are three accessories you **make for yourself:**
push sticks
dust collector
table extensions

On-off switch

You must be able to shut off the saw by touch, and you should be able to shut it off by banging the switch with your body or knee. When something unexpected occurs in the middle of a sawing operation, you'll need to stop the saw without being able to take your eyes off the blade or your hand off the workpiece.

The on-off switch should be brightly colored, even fluorescent. It should be mounted in easy reach under the left front edge of the saw table. The off button should be a large pad that behaves like a hair trigger.

The first thing to do with a new saw is to stand at the machine and see if you can put your hand on the switch without any groping. Practice with your eyes closed, and practice hitting the switch with your thigh. You have to know where it is. An emergency is too late to be learning.

If the on-off switch on your saw is not well placed and you can move it, do so. If the off button is not totally easy to push, buy one that is.

Bright red off switch must be lifted to get at the on-button, but it can be turned off with a tap.

When you switch on...

When you switch any machine to **on**, position your hand so you can switch it **off** in a millisecond. Practice this maneuver and make it a habit. Flip the machine on and off again long before it comes up to full speed. If there is anything wrong — blade loose on the arbor, wood touching the blade — this is when it happens. You have to be in control.

Blade elevation and arbor tilt

The blade of a contractor saw goes up and down, and the arbor tilts, by way of rack-and-pinion gears. The racks are quadrants, and the pinions, or worm gears, connect to the hand wheels that you turn.

These mechanisms have built-in stops to limit their travel and to help return the saw to 90 degrees. The important stops are the 45 degree and 90 degree ones on the arbor tilt mechanism. Check the blade angle with a square, being sure to rest the square's blade against the saw plate, not against a carbide tooth. Adjust the stops accordingly and tighten their lock nuts.

To work smoothly and accurately, there shouldn't be any slop in the rack-and-pinion mechanisms. Most saws have eccentric bushings for taking the play out of the mechanism. To adjust the bushing, loosen the stop collar adjacent to the pinion or worm gear, then turn the eccentric. When it's tight, retighten the bushing.

Under the saw. The front handwheel raises the saw blade, while the side one tilts the saw arbor. The two steel rods connect the arbor-tilting trunnions.

To tighten the worm gear, clean the impacted crud off the parts, then loosen the collar at left and turn the nut .

Why not to tilt

The worm gear tilts the trunnion and the saw arbor. Two steel rods transmit the movement to the rear trunnion (below), which slides in a semicircular track.

The arbor-tilting rack drives a pair of semi-circular trunnions connected by two steel rods. The rods stabilize the mechanism and keep the moving parts in line. However, the shoulders on the two rods are all that hold the parts square and rigid. They're likely to twist when you tilt the arbor.

Sawdust and grease harden in the rack-and-pinion mechanism, making it stick. When you crank the handwheel hard enough to override the stickiness, you also stress the mechanism, throwing the connecting rods out of line. The arbor and saw blade do not return to their square position.

One remedy is to practice getting under the saw and realigning the mechanism, so you can do it it after every tilting setup. However, the remedy I prefer is to set up the saw so it is truly square, lock it down tight, and leave it there. To make bevel cuts, build jigs to hold the work while leaving the saw square (page 132).

Stress on the mechanism throws the rods out of line, preventing the arbor from returning to square.

Saw table

The saw table is the machine's fundamental reference. It corresponds to the face side on the wood. The rest of the saw's parts have to be aligned with the table, and all measurements of parallelism and right-angularity spring from it. To do accurate work, the saw table has to be flat.

The saw table is an iron casting that has been flattened at the factory. Cast iron moves, so it's entirely possible that your saw table was flat when it left the factory, but the metal has distorted since it was machined.

Flattening the table

Use a 24-inch straight edge to check the saw table for flatness. Check parallel to the table slots, and at right-angles to them. If you position an incandescent light on the far side of the table, you'll be able to see the deviation as a line of light underneath the straight edge. You can measure it with automotive feeler gauges. Hills and bumps require attention because they make the wood rock on the table.

You can remove a serious hill by grinding the metal with a belt sander or auto-body grinder, and you can take out a smaller one with a coarse diamond sharpening stone. Mark the metal

Check for flat with a long straight edge. Draw contour lines around the hills and bumps. This machine has a hill alongside the table opening.

Grind the hill down flat using a coarse diamond stone. Lubricate the stone with light oil or with water.

to be removed with a felt pen, as a series of rings like the contours on a map. Check your progress with a straight edge, and re-mark the metal to be removed after each check. Also check the table's edges for sharps and bumps, and remove them. Draw-file the edges to a small chamfer.

Hollow places are not a problem because the wood will bridge them without rocking.

Assessing twist

Twist means the surface has a slight propeller shape, with diagonally opposite corners high or low. You'll often hear woodworkers complain that their machine tables are twisted, but it's rarely true. The problem is much more likely to be bad setup, sloppy procedure, or twisted wood. To check the saw table for twist, sight across a pair of winding sticks, the same way you check wood for twist (page 21).

Once you do detect twist, the problem is deciding whether or not it really is a problem. A small amount of twist, 1/16 inch or less over a 20-inch span, won't affect the usual 6-inch wide workpiece. If you've got more twist than that, and if you normally saw wide pieces of wood, you might have a problem. If so, contact your dealer and look at it together.

You may be able to remove a small amount of twist by putting tension on the metal. Begin by bolting the saw base to a flat and level pad on the floor of the workshop. Then unbolt the saw table from the base. Make sure there are no high places interfering with how the table fastens to the base. Insert shims of metal or paper under the low spot, then bolt it down tight and check again.

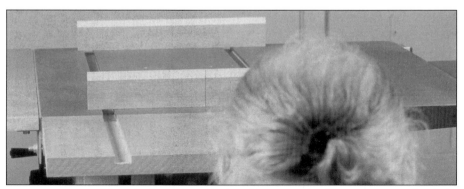

The winding sticks don't indicate any significant amount of twist in this saw table.

Aligning the arbor and table slots

Since the two slots milled into the table surface guide the miter gauge and some jigs, it's important that the blade run parallel to them. This means the saw arbor, on which the blade mounts, has to be at right angles to the slots.

Before checking the alignment of the saw arbor, mount a carbide-tipped blade on it. Raise the blade to its highest position, and make it square to the surface of the table.

Lay a 24-inch straight edge on the face of the saw blade. Make sure it rests squarely on the plate itself, missing the carbide teeth.

Now measure the distance from both ends of the straight edge to one of the table slots. If the two measurements are the same, the blade is parallel to the slots, which means the arbor is correctly aligned. If the two measurements do not agree, loosen three of the four bolts that fasten the arbor trunnion to the underside of the saw table. Use a mallet or a hammer and a block of wood to tap the trunnion one way or the other. When the measurements are equal, tighten the bolts. Then check again, in case the act of tightening the bolts threw the arbor out of alignment. Once you have aligned the arbor, it should not need further adjustment.

Arbor runout

The saw arbor is supposed to rotate smoothly, without any perceptible wobble or bounce. In circular shafts, deviation from perfect rotation is called runout. While a machinist can measure runout, you can't do it with the usual woodworking tools. You can, however, diagnose runout by assessing how well the saw cuts. Once you have gone through the complete set-up routine, if it won't saw straight and clean with any of several different blades, you'd be right to suspect arbor runout. Discuss it with your dealer and see if he'll exchange the machine or replace the parts.

Disconnect the power

Before you remove the table insert to work on the saw, whether to change blades, re-install the splitter, or for clean-up and maintenance, **disconnect the saw from its electrical supply.** It is not safe to rely on the on-off switch. Unplug it.

Lay the straight edge against the saw plate, between the carbide teeth.

Measure from the straight edge to the saw slot. To create a positive stop, put the stock of the square against the wall of the slot.

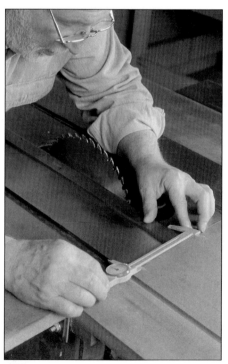

As an alternative, make the measurement with a dial caliper spanning the distance from slot to straight edge.

Splitter

The splitter or riving knife prevents kickback by keeping the newly sawn workpiece or falling board out of contact with the back edge of the saw blade. If the wood were to contact the back edge of the blade, it would be thrown toward the operator with tremendous speed and force. Practically all kickback accidents can be attributed to not using the splitter.

A correctly designed splitter is a metal fin the same thickness as the saw blade. It closely follows the curve of the blade, with a gap of about 1/4 inch, and it rises and falls along with the blade. Kickback is practically impossible on a saw equipped with a properly designed and installed splitter.

Unfortunately, most table saws have a splitter that's part of the blade guard, made of metal that is too thin. US manufacturers recently have added a set of spring-loaded anti-kickback fingers on top of the splitter. This design means the splitter can't be used in some situations.

The splitter is an essential piece of safety apparatus.

If your saw doesn't have one, buy an aftermarket splitter, or make one that you can mount behind the blade.

Without a splitter, the wood can contact the rising teeth at the back of the blade, and kick back.

The splitter keeps the wood away from the back of the blade.

Delta *aftermarket splitter has quick-remove knob.*

DeWalt *splitter rises and falls.*

Look for an aftermarket splitter that is the same thickness as a standard carbide-tipped saw blade. Some types mount to the arbor trunnion with a quick-release knob. A separate splitter works better than a combination guard-and-splitter.

To adjust the splitter, raise the blade so you can lay a metal straight edge on the saw plate, between the teeth. The straight edge should just touch the face of the splitter, on either side. To align it, find the mounting bolts and adjust them.

To check the splitter, rip 4 inches down the center of a 6-inch-wide board. Shut the saw off, then lower the blade and feed the board into the splitter. You'll see whether the splitter centers in the cut, and you'll feel any misalignment.

Antikickback pawls

To test the antikickback pawls, saw part-way through a piece of wood and turn the saw off. Then try to pull the wood straight back. The pawls should dig into the wood and prevent it from moving toward you. If they slip, file the pawls to sharp points.

Antikickback pawls are a recent addition to American table saws. They aren't found on European machines. They have three deficiencies. First, you can't withdraw the workpiece once it has come into contact with the pawls. Second, mounting pawls on the splitter prevents designing a splitter that rises and falls with the blade. Finally, the pawls touch the surface of the wood. Eventually they will catch in the kerf or in a split in the wood, and hang it up.

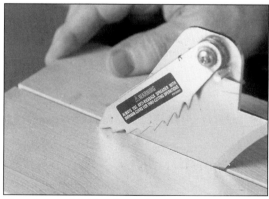

Test the antikickback pawls with the saw turned off. They should dig into the wood and prevent it from moving back toward the operator.

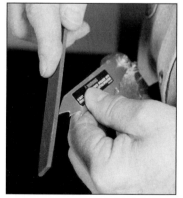

File the antikickback pawls to chisel points so they will catch the wood.

Blade guard

A correctly designed saw guard should cover the blade while permitting easy access for the workpiece. It should not touch the workpiece, because eventually the wood will hang up as a result of this contact. It should not impede the passage of the workpiece, nor make it difficult to use hold-downs and push sticks. And it must not block the operator's view.

The guard shipped with most saws interferes with the easy passage of workpiece and push stick past the saw blade, or it blocks the operator's view of the work, or both. The best of the standard guards fails when you try to rip a narrow slice off the wood. You have to lift the guard high above the work, because you can't bring it right close to the fence.

Operating the saw without a guard is not the answer. The answer is to purchase an aftermarket guard that works properly, and learn how to get the most out of it.

Aftermarket guards

Adding adequate guards to your table saw increases your investment in machinery. These additional investments are not optional, they are necessary. The guard may cost as much as one-third to one-half the price of the saw itself. There are two basic styles of aftermarket blade guard.

Metal basket or cowl,

Clear plastic plate or box.

Guards made from heavy Lexan plastic have the advantage that you can see through them, though manufacturers often defeat this advantage with safety stickers.

Some guards are mounted so they hover over the workpiece, and some ride up onto the workpiece. The hovering style is better, because it can't get caught on the wood. There are three ways to mount an aftermarket blade guard:

Right-mounted,

Left-mounted,

Ceiling mounted.

Right-mounted guards are carried by a U-shaped arm mounted far to the right of the blade and arching over the saw table and fence. Although this approach solves many guarding problems, it may limit how close you can bring the fence to the blade. Nevertheless, a right-mounted guard gives enough clearance for a wide piece of plywood to pass between fence and blade, and a clear left side.

Left-mounted guards generally have a demountable bracket on the left side of the saw blade. You can adjust the guard to leave space for a push stick between it and the fence. This type of guard limits the width of the workpiece on the left, so large sheets have to be rough-cut before sawing.

Ceiling-mounted guards do away with the support apparatus that interferes with the workpiece. However, you have to decide where the table saw is going to live and leave it there. The ceiling mount also has to be easy to take down, because otherwise it will prevent you from using tenoning jigs and other accessories. While manufacturers don't sell a ceiling-mounted apparatus, it's easy to convert most guards.

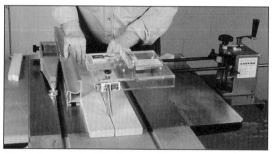

The left-mounted Brett guard is a heavy Lexan box that covers the blade. It carries its own antikickback device, but requires a separate splitter.

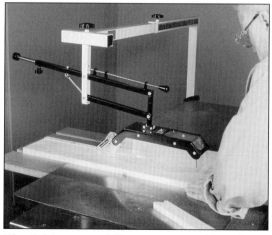

The right-mounted Biesemeyer guard is a plastic and metal basket on a long U-shaped arm. It also requires a separate splitter.

This basket-style guard converts easily from a right-mounted arm to a ceiling-mounted bracket. It can be screwed or clamped in place.

Fence

The fence guides the wood parallel to the saw blade. It moves to accommodate different widths of cut, and it has to lock down tight. The fence must also be:

parallel to the saw blade after adjustment;

adjustable in length according to the cut being made.

You'll find argument about both of these points in other table saw handbooks.

Regarding parallel, some people advocate making the fence toe out from the blade by 1/64 inch or more. They imagine that this reduces the risk of kickback. However, any deviation from parallel is bound to bring one side of the blade into contact with the spinning teeth. The result will be ragged fibers on the surface of the wood, an inaccurate cut, and increased risk of kickback. A splitter is the correct solution to kickback.

Regarding fence length, it depends on the material being cut. Plywood is stable and does not distort, so it can be sawn with a full-length fence extending right across the saw table. Solid wood is liable to distort while it is being cut. It might move into the blade, or it might curl away. Therefore the fence should stop just beyond the point of incision. Otherwise, the work could bind between blade and fence, the cut would become inaccurate, and the situation would be ripe for kickback.

Aftermarket fence has easy length adjustment, as well as screwdriver adjustments for square and parallel.

Aligning the fence

The fence must be square to the saw table. Most fences have an adjustment for squareness, but if yours doesn't, you can insert shims. The fence must remain parallel to the saw blade. It must not toe in or out.

It's normal to align the fence after aligning the saw arbor to the table slots (page 34). Unplug the machine. Raise the saw blade to its highest elevation. Begin by making the fence square to the saw table, then adjust for parallel. Lay your straight edge against the blade plate and clamp it to the saw table. Next, move the fence to within an inch or so of the straight edge, and measure the gap at both ends, using a rigid metal ruler, not a tape measure. If the gap is the same at both ends, the fence and saw plate are parallel. If the gap is not the same, work with the adjustments built into the fence to bring it into line.

Once you've made the adjustment, unlock the fence and move it, then bring it back and lock it. It should remain parallel to the blade. If there's a built-in indicator, zero it, so fence-setting becomes an onboard operation that doesn't require a tape measure. After checking a few cuts, you'll become adept at setting the fence to a precise dimension.

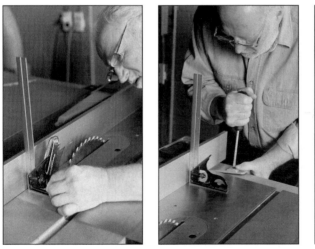

Set the square on the saw table and bring it up to the fence to check for squareness. Adjust the fence until it is perfectly square.

To adjust for parallel, lay the straight edge against the blade plate and measure to the fence at either end. The measurements should be the same.

Table insert

The table insert fills in the opening around the saw blade. Removing the insert gives you access to change the blade. The insert must fit level and tight in its opening. It is never safe to run the saw without an insert. Before you remove the insert, always unplug the machine.

Most saws come with a metal table insert. The insert should have four Allen screws that allow you to bring it exactly flush with the table surface. Make this adjustment with the aid of a steel straight edge. Once set, if the insert begins to interfere with the workpiece, unplug the saw and see what is the cause. It could be a bit of crud packed up underneath, or it could be that vibration has moved the Allen screws.

On most inserts, the gap alongside the blade is wider than it needs to be. If you want to reduce it you can buy a plastic insert or make a wooden one, but don't forget to include a slot for the splitter.

You can buy special wide-slot inserts for dadoing, or you can use a wooden or plastic insert that has no precut slot. These allow you to raise the dado set through the insert, creating a tight and precise slot.

Four Allen screws resting on pads cast into the saw table level the insert. The white block at lower left is the splitter mount.

To level the insert, set a straight edge across it and turn each Allen screw. Make sure the insert doesn't rock.

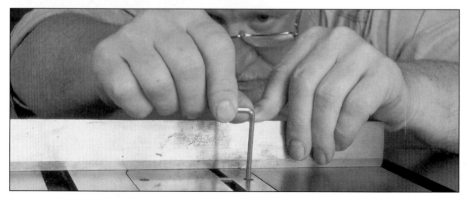

Making inserts

As an alternative to buying a new insert, you can trace the standard item onto 1/2-in hardwood or plywood and cut it out. If hardwood, choose quarter-sawn for stability, and if plywood, choose a uniform laminate like Baltic birch. To make the insert fit the opening precisely, clamp the metal one to the wood and pattern-rout around it with a flush-cutting bit. Start with blanks sawn to the exact overall length and width of the original.

Making the blade slot in a wooden insert is not as simple as raising the regular saw blade up through the wood. Most saws don't have enough clearance to allow you to fully seat the unslotted insert in the first place. You'll need an 8-inch blade, or the outside cutter from a dado set, to start the slot. Before attempting this operation, lock the insert in place by clamping a piece of wood across the top of the saw table.

To level the wooden insert, drill pilot holes and thread regular Allen screws into them, same as on a metal insert.

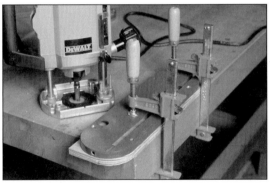

Use the original insert as a pattern for routing a new wooden insert. Rout one quadrant at a time, using a flush-cutting bit with a top-mounted ball-bearing.

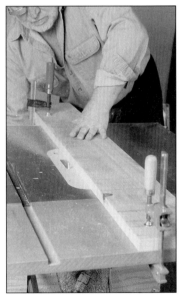

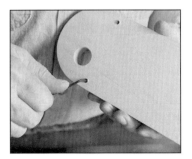

Allen screws will self-thread into holes a hair larger than their own root diameter.

Lock the wooden insert in place by clamping a board across the saw table. Raise the dado blade up through it.

Miter gauge

The miter gauge allows you to crosscut wood with square ends, and you can set it to crosscut at any angle between 45 degrees and 90 degrees, right or left. To prepare it for accurate work, screw a wooden fence to it. To make parts to a known length, or multiples to the same length, clamp a stop block to the miter gauge fence.

The miter gauge typically consists of a metal casting that pivots on a metal bar, which runs in one of the table grooves. The face of the miter gauge has holes in it so you can attach a wooden fence. Fasten the wooden fence with screws driven from the operator side. Make the auxiliary face at least an inch thick, and long enough to extend at least 6 inches to the outboard side and past the blade on the inboard side. Saw the fence to exact length after you screw it to the gauge body.

Miter gauges: Standard Delta miter gauge, left, and aftermarket FastTrak gauge.

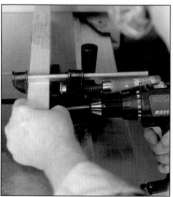

Screw a wooden fence *to the miter gauge.*

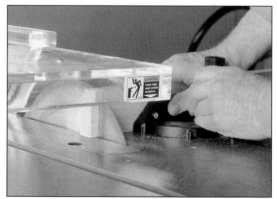

Saw the fence to length.

For accurate work, the bar has to be a snug fit in the table grooves. If it is too loose, tighten the fit with a bit of metal-working. Remove the bar from its slot and center-punch a series of dimples along one edge. The center punch makes little craters with raised walls. Draw-file the dimpled edge to fit the bar snugly into the table slot, with no side-to-side play. If working on one edge doesn't tighten the bar, do the other edge as well. As an alternative to metalworking, you can buy a replacement bar that has little adjustable blocks screwed into its edges. They're found in woodworking catalogs.

Most miter gauges have a pointer for 90 degrees, with a screw stop you can set for a spot-on 90-degree cut. To adjust the stop, set the pointer at 90 degrees and make a test cut. Check the wood against your square to see whether it is 90 degrees. If not, adjust the screw stop and try again. Once you get the gauge stop adjusted so it cuts at 90 degrees, tighten the lock nut so you can return to the same setting.

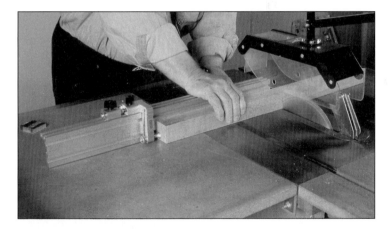

Aftermarket fences, like this Fast-Trak system, have a built-in flip-up stop block. With the stop block up you can cut one end square, then flip the stop down and make the second end square and to length.

Table extensions

Saws come with a relatively small table, but you can extend it to suit your work.

Some bench-top saws offer suitable table extensions, but for those that don't, you can build your own out of plywood. Use a buttress-and-glueblock construction, like the approach suggested for making jigs on page 126.

Contractor and cabinet saws usually come with a choice of right and left extensions, some made of sheet metal, some of cast iron, and some of MDF. A right-hand extension also involves extending the rightward travel of the fence, usually by replacing its guide rail. Some cabinet models also offer optional sliding tables.

It's helpful to extend the rear of the table, where the workpiece needs support after the cut has been made. An extension of about 12 inches here will make a big reduction in the amount of wood that ends up falling to the floor. Make the extension out of 3/4-inch or 1-inch sheet material. Since a rear table intersects the table slots, rout a continuation of the slots in it.

Extension tables should be exactly level and flush with the main saw table. Sheet-metal extensions and shop-made wooden ones may need diagonal braces to keep them level.

For ripping long stock, use roller stands or sawhorses to catch the workpiece on the outfeed side. Stands and rollers should be 1/8 inch to 1/4 inch below the level of the table, so the workpiece doesn't hang up.

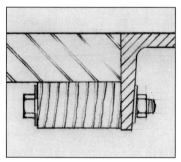

Glue oak rail to MDF extension table and trim it flush, then fasten the assembly to the saw table with two 5/16-inch bolts.

Routed slots continue table slots in rear extension.

Dust collection

The table saw throws a lot of dust and makes a lot of chips. It's not difficult to adapt a saw to a dust collection system. Some models have the beginnings of dust panels with exhaust ports, although none of them comes with a well designed dust system.

Bench-top saws and cabinet saws have enclosed bases, which may have dust ports built into them. Contractor-style saws are open at the bottom and back. It's usually best to connect the dust collection hose to the bottom of the saw base, and to make a wooden plate that fits closely around the motor and drive belts.

One way to connect the dust collection hose is to make a bottom plate out of 1/2-inch plywood. Find a plumbing fixture that will accept the flexible dust-collector hose, and mount it in the middle of the plywood plate. Then drill holes and screw the plywood to the underside of the saw.

A plywood back plate traps sawdust and helps it enter the dust-collection hose. The plate shown would interfere with the drive belt if this saw were ever tilted, which it is not. If you intend to tilt your saw, modify the plate to clear the drive belt.

Maintenance

The dust and pitch thrown by the saw blade plays havoc with the mechanism under the saw table. The heavy grease that the manufacturer slathers onto the moving parts makes it worse. The grease is necessary to prevent rust while the saw emigrates from their overseas factory to your shop. But once you start to saw wood, the grease is a dust magnet.

The remedy is to clean all the grease off the moving parts, by washing with solvent during the initial setup of the machine. Then keep these parts clean and lubricated with a light machine oil.

The everyday job of maintaining your table saw is primarily a matter of keeping it clean. Sweep dust and chips off the saw table, and sweep up around the saw at the end of every work session. Sweep and vacuum chips and sawdust from inside the saw base.

To keep the saw's cast-iron surfaces from rusting, wipe them down with a very slightly oily rag. "Very slightly oily" means a rag that has had a few drops of oil squeezed onto it, a few days ago. Do this about once a week. To clean rust, spills and pitch deposits off the table, rub it down with Scotch-Brite and light oil. Lubricate the locking mechanism on the fence with light machine oil, once a month.

The only way to keep track of blade changes, lubrication and maintenance is to keep a written log for each machine.

Keep a log if you want to keep track of maintenance schedules.

Sweep dust and chips off the saw table.

Push sticks

Wooden push sticks are an essential but expendable table saw accessory that you make for yourself. Two push sticks should be on the saw table at all times, one on the right and one on the left, ready to pick up and use. The saw is not set up until you equip it with a pair of push sticks.

Push sticks are easy to make. The right-angled notch in the end of the stick is called a bird's-mouth. To make the bird's-mouth, simply hold the stick alongside the end of a board, trace the shape of the board, and cut it out. For normal woodworking, make push sticks out of 3/4-inch wood. In special situations, such as when ripping a narrow slice of wood, make a thin push stick out of thin wood.

Although you can buy plastic push sticks, and many woodworking handbooks offer elaborate designs for them, it is pointless to make anything but the simplest kind, because they are going to get chewed up. If you invest more than is necessary in an elaborate or expensive push stick, you might hesitate to let it go into the saw blade. Yet the purpose of the push stick is to keep control of the workpiece at the end of the cut, while keeping fingers out of harm's way. If the stick gets chewed up in the process, that's to be expected.

Using push sticks, page 75.

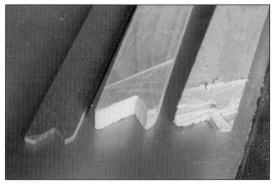

Make narrow push sticks of tempered Masonite, regular ones out of 1x2. Expect them to get chewed up.

Lay out the push stick by tracing the corner of a block of wood.

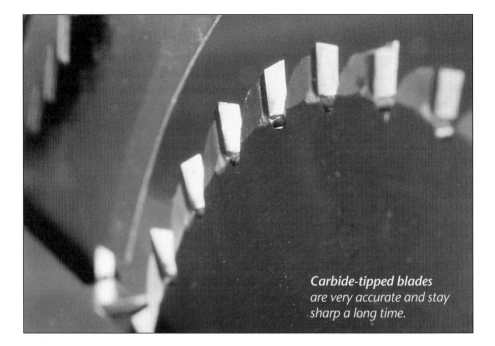

Carbide-tipped blades are very accurate and stay sharp a long time.

CHAPTER 4

Saw Blades

Modern saw blades have teeth formed from little blocks of tungsten carbide brazed to a flat steel plate. This material is so hard, sharp and long-wearing that old-style spring-set steel blades are obsolete, and have all but disappeared from the marketplace. Tungsten-carbide tipped blades are so good that you no longer need different blades for ripping, cross-cutting and sawing sheet materials. For me one style of blade, the alternate-top-bevel or ATB, will do all the jobs.

The quantum leap represented by the tungsten carbide tipped blade can't be overstated. Compared to sprung-set steel blades, it's like the leap from propeller aircraft to jet engines. The quality produced by any carbide-tipped blade far exceeds what you could get from the best all-steel blade.

The diagrams in this chapter show the parts of the saw blade and some of the things you'll encounter when you shop for blades. However, the most important consideration is price. Saw blades are difficult to manufacture, and high-quality blades are expensive. Since you can't buy and test them all, you have to trust that you get what you pay for, and in my experience, you generally do.

Blade diameter

Saws are defined by the largest blade diameter they will accept. Blade diameter is measured from tooth tip to tooth tip, across the center of the blade. Most saws accept blades that are 10 inches in diameter, although some bench-top saws go no larger than 8 inches. You can run a smaller blade, but it won't be able to cut as deep as the standard blade.

Blade plate

The saw plate is the steel disc of the blade. It must be flat and smooth. A lot of manufacturing money goes into surface-grinding and shaping the plate. The arbor hole, expansion slots, gullets and tooth sockets usually are laser-cut so as not to introduce stress and distortion.

Expansion slots. A working blade generates heat, which makes the metal expand. The expansion slots help it stay flat.

Gullets. The gullet is the space between two adjacent teeth. The gullets carry the waste out of the cut. Sawdust expands to about three times the volume of the wood that made it; when the gullets fill up with sawdust, the blade can't cut any more. The volume of the gullets therefore limits how fast you can feed wood into the saw. Since modern saws have ample gullets, you'll never come near this limit even with a power feeder.

Arbor hole. The standard saw arbor is 5/8 inch in diameter, and the hole in the middle of the saw blade must also be 5/8 inch. It has to be a tight fit.

Kerf

The kerf is the cut in the wood created by the blade. A **standard-kerf** blade makes a kerf that is 1/8 inch wide. This means that the tungsten carbide blocks are ground to create a 1/8-inch (.125 inch) kerf, but they are mounted onto a disk that is about .09 inch thick. A **thin-kerf** blade makes a cut 3/32 inch (.09375 inch) wide. Its saw plate is about .075 inch thick. Because the kerf is thin you need less saw power and you conserve wood.

Teeth

The **carbide tip** or block is what does the actual sawing. There are different carbide compounds, but there's no way to tell the difference. Whatever the tooth geometry, for smooth results, the carbide must be smooth and sharp, so take a magnifying glass when you shop. Under 4x magnification, you shouldn't be able to see any scratches or chips where the carbide faces meet. When comparing two blades, check the size of the carbide blocks. Bigger is better, because the blade can be sharpened more times before it finally wears out.

Pitch. The pitch of a blade is the distance between tooth points. At a given diameter the pitch depends upon the number of teeth, so the word has come to mean tooth count as well. The number of teeth on a 10-inch blade commonly varies between 25 and 80. While it's generally accepted that more teeth leave a finer surface, and fewer teeth cut more quickly, the differences are minute.

Hook. Imagine a line drawn through the center of the saw blade to the tip of a tooth. The hook is the angle between the front face of the tooth and this radial line; when the front face of the tooth falls right on a radius, the hook is zero. Hook affects the quality and aggressiveness of the cut. A positive hook of 5 to 15 degrees produces the best results in wood.

Top bevel. The top bevel is the angle made by the tooth's cutting edge, measured across the thickness of the blade. A small amount of top bevel helps the tooth sever the wood, making a cleaner cut. Top bevel typically varies between 0 degrees (**flat top**) and 15 degrees, and is limited by the characteristics of the carbide alloy — too much top bevel makes a fragile tooth. Recent advances in carbide processing permit increasing the top bevel to about 25 degrees, producing **steep top bevel** teeth. These blades reduce raggedness on the cut. A flat top tooth with its corners top-beveled at 45 degrees is called a **triple-chip grind (TCG)**.

Top clearance. Imagine a line tangent to the blade's circle at the tip of a tooth. The top surface of the tooth has to fall away from this line, or the tip can't cut. Top clearance of about 5 degrees is typical.

Side clearance. Most blades have a small amount of clearance between the cutting edge and the side of the carbide tooth. The clearance reduces overheating, but smaller clearances produce the cleanest cuts. So-called "planer" blades may have zero side clearance.

Face angle. The front face of the tooth makes an angle measured from the plate of the blade. When the angle is 90 degrees, the tooth is called flat-faced. Angles up to about 15 degrees make a sharper tooth and a cleaner cut. Face angle alternates right and left, along with the top bevel.

Blade configurations

Manufacturers tailor their blades to different purposes by combining various tooth patterns. When the sawdust settles, there are five basic blade configurations.

Flat top

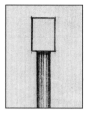

Teeth with flat tops, that is, with 0 degrees of top bevel, act like planes or chisels. They peel the wood fibers away. A blade designed for ripping could have all flat-top teeth. However, the flat-top tooth is more commonly used in combination with other shapes. When used in combinations, flat-top teeth are called rakers. A flat-top tooth leaves a flat-bottomed kerf.

Alternate top bevel (ATB)

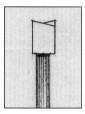

The teeth are top-beveled alternately right and left. Their sharp points act like little knives, severing the wood fibers on either side of the kerf. Although ATB teeth were designed specifically for cross-cutting, they are an excellent general purpose blade. An ATB blade does not make a flat-bottomed kerf. Instead, it leaves a vee profile, deeper at the edges than in the center.

Steep alternate top bevel (SATB)

The teeth are beveled alternately with extra-sharp points. These general-purpose blades sever the veneers in plywood, producing a cleaner cut, though they do not make a flat-bottomed kerf.

ATB with raker (ATBR)

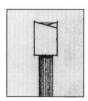

For a true general-purpose blade, manufacturers combine the ATB configuration with chip-clearing raker teeth. Usually the teeth are grouped, with four ATB teeth followed by a single flat-top raker. Since the raker usually is not as high as the tips of the top-beveled teeth, an ATBR blade does not make a flat-bottomed kerf.

Triple-chip grind (TCG)

A TCG blade alternates flat-top teeth with triple-chip teeth, which project minutely beyond the flat-top teeth. This configuration nibbles away at hard, brittle and abrasive materials, such as medium-density fiberboard and laminate-faced particle boards. Some people prefer TCG blades for plywood and veneers as well. A TCG blade does not make a flat-bottomed kerf.

Changing blades

To change the saw blade, follow these steps:

Unplug the saw and remove the table insert. Raise the blade to its full height.

Remove the blade. Most saws come with two wrenches and you should use both. The smaller wrench grips two flats on the arbor, while the larger one grips the blade nut. First, set the smaller wrench on the arbor. Second, set the larger wrench on the arbor nut and loosen the nut. Third, remove the arbor nut wrench and spin the nut free with your fingers. Let it drop into the palm of your hand.

Before you replace the blade, check the arbor and threads for crud, and clean it off.

Fit the new blade onto the arbor and be sure the teeth are pointing toward the infeed edge of the table.

Replace the arbor nut. Examine the nut and see whether it has one side that is clearly flatter than the other. If so, this side goes toward the saw blade. Spin the nut finger tight. Then re-set both wrenches and firmly tighten the nut.

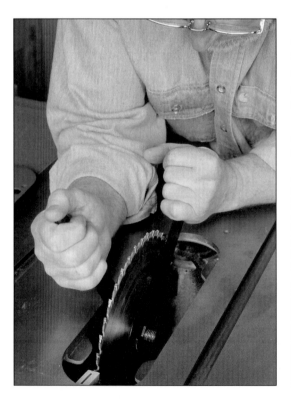

Tighten and loosen the saw blade using the two wrenches that came with it. Spin the nut off with your fingers. Keep your hand cupped under the nut so it doesn't drop into the dust hose. When you tighten it, make it snug but don't apply your full strength to it.

Always pull the plug

Every time you change the blade on any table saw, you must disconnect the saw from its electrical supply. Pull the plug. Don't rely on the on-off switch.

The marketing of saw blades

Modern carbide-tipped saw blades are extremely good, and you can expect to get the level of quality that you pay for. However, in order to gain market share, blade manufacturers make all sorts of claims. They extol special coatings, specially shaped teeth that will cut better in this material or that material, and special gullet profiles that limit kickback or control feed rate. It's extremely difficult to evaluate these claims, some make sense and some don't, so keep your grain of salt at hand.

Blade stiffeners

Blade stiffeners are accurately machined oversized washers. They will stabilize a thin-kerf blade in hard materials like oak or maple. The drawback is that they limit the rise of the blade, reducing the depth of cut. If the geometry of the saw arbor is out of whack, stiffeners won't help it, nor will they do anything for a blade that needs sharpening. In the work I do, I've not found them necessary.

Chip-limiting blade

There are no absolutes about tooth shape and gullet design. The shapes have evolved to suit manufacturing technologies and users' needs. This has given rise to blades with tooth-stiffening blocks, chip-limiting ears, and novel antikickback profiles. I haven't seen anything that convinces me these designs are an improvement, but they probably do no harm either. You will have to judge for yourself.

Power feeders

Another industrial device now finding its way to the small shop is the power feeder. These devices consist of a variable speed motor driving a head that carries feed wheels. The wheels have soft plastic tires, which straddle the saw blade and push the workpiece. The head is set at a slight angle so the tires press the workpiece hard into the fence. A power feeder can produce consistently accurate results. The trouble is, the cheap units don't work very well, while good ones cost half as much as the saw itself, or more.

Special-purpose cutterheads

There are two useful special-purpose cutters for the table saw:

the dado head,

the molding head.

Both of these are shaping tools — they change the profile of the wood, but they don't sever it into two pieces.

Dado head

A dado cutterhead consists of two outside saw blades mounted with one or more chippers in between. Most dado heads are smaller than a regular saw blade, usually 8 inches in diameter. The chippers, which usually have as few as two or as many as eight teeth, come in precise thickness, so some combination of outside blades and chippers will make up whatever width you require. For fine variations on the standard widths, you can also insert shims between the chippers.

A dado head cuts a **groove**, which runs with the grain; a **housing**, which is a groove across the grain; and a **rebate**, which is a right-angled cutout along the edge of the wood.

Molding head

The major manufacturers sell molding heads designed to fit the arbor of the saw. Most of them accept three-knife sets, and a reasonable variety of knife profiles are available. While a table saw can't do all the work of a router table or a shaper, it can do some shaping very well.

Three-knife molding head, made by Delta, comes with a variety of knife sets. Page 119.

This Forrest dado *set consists of two outside blades (only one is shown), with five inside cutters of various widths.*

Blade maintenance

For good performance, keep your saw blades clean and sharp. Gum, pitch and scorched bits of wood on the teeth will get in the way of the cut. The amount of buildup depends on the type of wood being sawn, but for accurate work, clean the blade more often.

To clean the blade, remove it from the saw and lay it in a 12-inch pizza pan. Soak it with a small amount of mineral spirits or paint thinner, and scrub it with a stiff bristle brush or a brass bristle brush. Oven-cleaning spray will dissolve stubborn deposits. Dry the blade before you reinstall it.

Because carbide wears so well, it's difficult to decide when to resharpen. Let the quality of the cut be your guide. It's likely to be a long time between sharpenings, years in an amateur shop. When a clean blade won't produce the surface you want, it's time to send the blade out for resharpening.

Incorrect sharpening will destroy an expensive blade. It has to be done by a precise machine using lubricated grinding, not by hand or by dry-grinding. This is why you cannot resharpen carbide yourself, and why many small sharpening shops are not equipped for it either. If you want to use a local sharpening service, find out exactly what they plan to do with your blade before they go ahead. And if you want to sidestep the problem altogether, send the blade back to the manufacturer for resharpening. If he does not offer a sharpening service, ask him to recommend one, or ask the people who sold the blade to you.

Clean the saw blade with solvent and a stiff bristle or brass brush in a 12-inch pizza pan.

Look at the end to see what it is. From top, flat-sawn ash that is heart side up, quarter-sawn pine, 3/4-inch cabinet-grade plywood faced with red oak veneer, 5/8-inch medium-density fiberboard (MDF).

CHAPTER 5

Wood and Working With It

We use the table saw for cutting two types of material: solid wood, and man-made sheet materials made from wood. From a sawing and woodworking point of view, these two kinds of materials are quite different.

Solid wood, which includes hardwoods and softwoods, has a grain structure. Because of its structure, wood is liable to distort while it is being sawn.

Man-made sheet materials include plywood, particleboard, medium-density fiberboard (MDF), high-density fiberboard (Masonite), Aspenite, and siding such as T1-11. None of these materials has an internal grain structure like that of solid wood. Although plywood and MDF may be covered with a face veneer, the veneer's grain direction doesn't say anything about internal structure. None of these materials is likely to distort while being sawn.

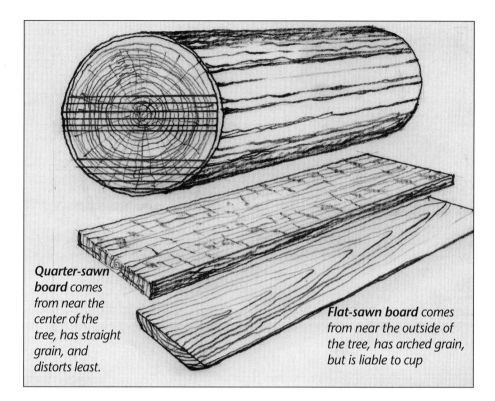

Quarter-sawn board comes from near the center of the tree, has straight grain, and distorts least.

Flat-sawn board comes from near the outside of the tree, has arched grain, but is liable to cup

It ain't plastic

Wood grows in trees, and because of the tree's desire to stand tall in the sun, wood has an internal structure. Unlike plastic, it's not the same in every direction. A board is a bundle of fibers (the **grain**) that run the same direction as the tree trunk. This is why wood splits along the grain, but not across it. The long fibers change direction to follow curves in the trunk of the tree, to support branches, and in response to the tree's growing conditions. If the tree grew leaning, the wood from one side of the trunk will be different from the wood on the other side. If the tree had to twist to remain in the sunlight, the grain will also twist.

When the tree trunk is sawn into boards, the wood contains about an equal weight of water and wood. Seasoning wood is the process of removing the water, or most of it. As the wood dries, it also shrinks, but it doesn't shrink uniformly.

If you look at the end of a board such as oak or ash, you'll see the curve of the annual rings. Each complete ring represents a year of growth in the life of the tree. The greatest amount of shrinkage occurs along the curve of the rings,

Hardwood

Softwood

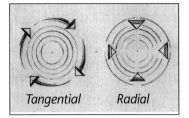

Tangential   Radial

that is, **tangentially**. Only about half as much occurs from one ring to the next, that is, **radially**. Almost no shrinkage occurs along the length of the wood, that is, **longitudinally**. The difference between tangential and radial shrinkage is called the **shrinkage differential**. This shrinkage difference is responsible for all distortion in wood.

Seasoned wood may show any of four kinds of distortion:

Cup.
The board is hollow across its width.

Bow
The board is flat in width but curves like a hill in the road.

Spring, or crook
The board is flat in width but curves like the bend in a river.

Twist
The board is shaped like an airplane propeller.

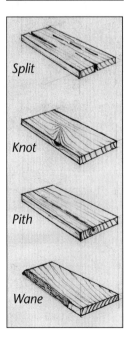

Cup

Bow

Spring

Twist

Split

Knot

Pith

Wane

In addition, you'll commonly encounter a number of typical defects, which you can saw around. These include:

Splits
Deep cracks running with the grain.

Knots
Where a branch grew.

Pith
The center of the tree, probably unstable.

Waney edge
The irregular outside of the tree.

Defects and distortion can be minimized by cutting the wood narrower or shorter, or both. However, some planks of wood remain distorted no matter how small you cut them. In those cases, you're holding firewood — burn it.

Harvesting the wood

When a factory processes wood, it's all treated the same — it goes in one end and comes out the other. As an amateur woodworker or builder, or small-shop cabinetmaker, you're not stuck with these economic necessities. You can take the time to make the most of the wood you've got.

The process of wood selection is interesting, it is time-consuming, but it always pays off in a better looking and stronger project. You can not only choose which board goes where, but also which part of each board. With your parts list at hand, go over all your wood with tape measure and chalk. Mark out all of the wood you expect to need. This process is called **harvesting.**

If the wood is rough, start by jointing one side and planing the other to maximum thickness, so you can really see what you've got. Begin harvesting by chalk-marking any defects you'll eliminate from the wood. While you may be tempted to save wood by sawing close to a knot, don't. The wood is liable to be distorted for several inches on either side. Cut out the pith because it tends to distort severely.

Once you have marked out all the defects, lay out the parts you need in order to harvest the most attractive wood figure. You don't have to stick with the existing edges of the boards. You can lay out parts on the diagonal if that's the way the grain runs.

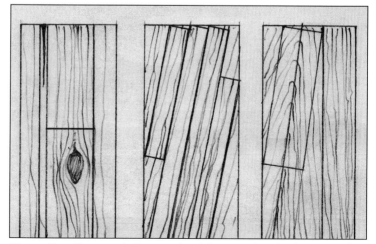

Harvesting the wood. Cut out the defects and make the most of the good material that remains.

Breakdown and dimensioning

We use the table saw in two different ways, at two different stages of woodworking:

as a **breakdown** tool,

as a **dimensioning** tool.

During breakdown, you're starting with large, heavy and often rough pieces of wood, or full sheets of manufactured board. The objective is to cut them down into manageable pieces. Saw these pieces close to size, about 1/2 inch longer and wider, to permit final cuts to precise size.

At breakdown, the wood doesn't have a face side or a face edge. You have look and decide which side of the board to plant on the saw table and which edge to run against the saw fence. Since you don't have accurate reference surfaces with which to guide the cut, you can't expect accurate results.

In between breakdown and dimensioning comes the process of putting a face side and a face edge on each piece of wood (page 64). Once the wood has a face side and a face edge, you can saw it to precise length and width, and you can plane it to precise thickness. However, until you have given it a face side and face edge, wood cannot be precisely dimensioned. In fact, preparing the wood properly and meticulously is the key to accuracy.

During dimensioning, after you have given the wood a face side and a face edge, you don't have to make any decisions about its orientation. The face side always goes down on the saw table. The face edge always goes against the fence or miter gauge. Because the wood has a face side and a face edge, it's possible to saw it to a precise size, with accuracy and certainty.

What to rough-cut first

When you rough out pieces of wood, you have to decide which cuts to make first. The general strategy depends on whether you're sawing solid wood or plywood. In solid wood, you try to harvest the best figure and color, and avoid the defects. In sheet materials, you're trying to achieve the most economical use of the board. You can get a computer program to help optimize sheet-goods breakdown.

For solid wood, the normal breakdown sequence is to cross-cut to rough length, rip to straighten one edge, then rip to finished width. This sequence will vary according to what you're making and exactly how you plan to harvest the parts you need from the boards you have. There is nothing wrong with ripping first, if that's what's necessary to get the parts you want.

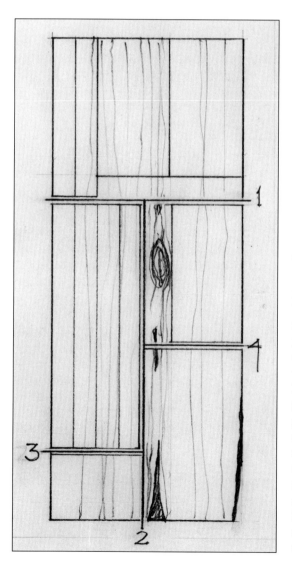

For plywood and other man-made sheet materials, the normal breakdown sequence is to make the longest cut or cuts first, keeping the larger piece of material between the blade and fence.

There are two grades of particle board, structural and industrial. Structural is for building houses, while industrial is a higher grade for making furniture and cabinets. The structural particle board you find at the home center comes in 4x8 sheets, while industrial-grade particle board is always an inch larger. This is so the worker can make his own straight edges, and still end up with a full sheet. You can get industrial-grade boards from wholesalers and dealers in specialty ply-woods.

Creating the face side and face edge

To do accurate work, the next step after roughing out the parts is creating a face side and a face edge on each piece. Accurate sawing depends on reference surfaces that can bear on the saw table and against the saw fence. Without accurate reference surfaces, you cannot do accurate work.

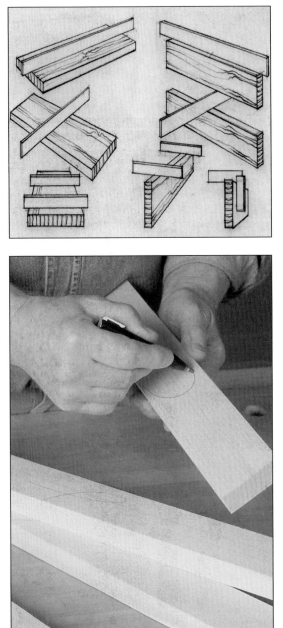

A **face side** has three characteristics:

flat in length,

flat in width,

doesn't twist.

A **face edge** has four characteristics:

flat in length,

flat in width,

doesn't twist,

square to the face side.

To assess the face side and the face edge, you need a straight edge, winding sticks, and square. How you achieve the face side and edge depends on what equipment you have. It can be done entirely with a hand plane, but the machine of choice is a jointer. When you use the jointer, always plane the face side first, mark it with a face side mark, then plane a face edge that is square to the face side and mark that. Face side and face edge marks record the actual condition of the wood. They're not hopeful declarations of intention.

Face side and face edge marks show that these two surfaces are flat and square.

Doing without a face side
and face edge

When you work without reference surfaces, and everyone does so at least part of the time, you can't expect to achieve spot-on accuracy. When you discover that the pieces of wood are not all the same size, or they don't all fit as precisely as you wanted, don't blame the saw. Remember that it was you who decided to proceed without creating a face side and face edge. If you want accuracy, you can't skip this process. It's that simple.

After breaking down the wood into manageable pieces you can saw it to size without the aid of a face side or a face edge. Simply choose the face that sits flattest on the saw table and declare it the face side, then choose the straighter of the two long edges, and declare it the face edge. Keep these two surfaces against the saw fences, and you will be working at a level of inaccuracy that's adequate for carpentry and for many household woodworking applications.

Many woodworkers believe they are preparing a face side by feeding wood through a thickness planer. The planer will do a good job of making both surfaces smooth and parallel to one another. However, any distortion that was present in the wood before planing to thickness will still be present afterward. Twist, in particular, twists right on through the planer, as does bow and, to a lesser extent, cup.

Managing distortion

Even after it has been properly dried, wood continues to expand and contract, in both width and thickness, in response to changes in the humidity of the atmosphere. The exchange of moisture between a board and the atmosphere is a dynamic process that can't be stopped. As a result, there's almost always a difference between the moisture content at the surface and deep inside the wood, and consequently, some amount of stress in the wood.

When you saw into solid wood, you become involved with its internal stresses. By cutting through the wood cells, you release the stress, and the wood immediately distorts in response. The sawn piece might curl one way or the other, it might twist, and it might break off. The difficulty is, you can't predict what might happen, and you can't prevent it.

Since you can't predict the distortion that may occur during the saw cut, you must anticipate it and accommodate it. This affects how you set up the saw, how you set the fence, where you stand, and how you control the wood during the cut. Each kind of defect represents a way for the sawing operation to go wrong, and requires a different response from you. You'll be able to work with almost any plank of wood, but how you work depends on your assessment of its defects.

Twist

To minimize twist, crosscut the board into short lengths. Of all defects, twist is the most troublesome. Twisted boards won't rest flat on the saw table, no matter which way around you turn them. Avoid buying twisted boards, but if you've got some, crosscut them into short pieces before you do anything else. You'll be able to extract some straight pieces at some length, but just how short depends on the board at hand. This is best done with a hand saw, portable circular saw or jig saw.

Cup

To minimize cup, rip the wood down the middle. Place it hollow side up on the saw table. If the two pieces are still too cupped to use, rip them still narrower.

Spring or crook

You can always crosscut crooked wood into shorter pieces,

but you cannot safely rip it without the aid of a guide board or a jig. If you need to use a long piece that has a crook, you can straighten it the same way you would handle waney-edged wood (below).

Bow

To minimize bow, crosscut the board into shorter lengths using a hand saw, portable circular saw or jig saw.

Knots

There are two kinds of knot — **tight**, and **loose**. A tight knot represents a branch that was alive when the tree was cut. It

Tight knot, top, is safe to saw, but loose knot, bottom, may go flying.

may have split during drying but it's clearly part of the surrounding wood and it won't fall out. Tight knots in softwood usually are pink or red in color. It's safe to saw wood that contains tight knots, provided the wood will hold together after the cut. However, if the wood does break apart at the knot, a piece of it is liable to be thrown by the saw. A loose knot represents a branch that died before the tree was cut. It's usually much darker than the surrounding wood and separated in places from its dark-lined hole. Knock it out with a hammer. Never saw through a loose knot. It will fly when cut in two, or else it will jam the saw. It's not dangerous to saw through a knot hole, as long as there is plenty of wood remaining to hold the board together.

Waney edge

The waney edge is the outside of the tree, with or without bark. A board with one waney edge can be sawn by keeping the sawn edge to the fence. A board with two waney edges can be sawn straight by fastening it with nails or screws to a guide board (page 89).

CHAPTER 6

Overview: Using the Saw

Every table saw operation requires you to pay attention to both saw setup and operator procedures. Exactly what you do about each point on the following list depends totally upon what you are sawing. However, in no event can you ignore any of the points.

Saw setup includes:

splitter,

fence,

blade height,

guard.

Operator procedure includes:

where to stand,

how to manage the cut.

If you've never used a table saw before, the first time you switch it on you're likely to be startled by the noise and wind. This can make it difficult for you to approach the saw. The first time you cut a piece of wood, the noise amplifies, and the wind becomes a cloud of sawdust.

To acquire good work habits, practice with the saw turned off. Rehearsing your moves is always a good way to focus your mind and prepare for success. Then, once you know where you're going to stand and how you're going to proceed, switch on the saw and repeat the maneuver live. Remember that learning to use a table saw doesn't have to be a demonstration of courage. If you're not sure, there's nothing wrong with shutting the saw off to rehearse.

If you've been using the table saw for a while, you've probably worked through any initial hesitation you might have experienced. You can use the basic instructions in this section to check your procedures and work habits.

Wear your safety glasses

Before you switch on the table saw, and every time you switch it on, be sure you are wearing safety glasses. Every hardware store and home center sells plastic goggles that surround your eyes. Most goggles are large enough to contain regular eyeglasses. As an alternative, you can buy prescription safety glasses with shatterproof plastic lenses and built-in side shields. Table saws throw up sawdust and particles of wood. There's no reason to risk getting any of this debris in your eyes.

Saw setup

It's worthwhile to cultivate a saw set-up routine that doesn't vary. Always check the details of the setup before every cut. Check that the saw table is clear of scrap, debris, chips and tools. Be sure that your push sticks are in place, close at hand.

Splitter

Use the splitter with every cut that severs the wood into two pieces. The splitter is essential to prevent kickback. You don't need the splitter for shaping cuts that don't divide the wood.

Fence

The details of how to manage the fence and miter gauge vary greatly with the material being cut and the type of cut being made. However, there are no cuts that can be made without either the saw fence or the miter gauge, or a jig guided by one of them. You can never cut freehand on the table saw.

Blade height

Everyone wants to know the correct blade height, but there isn't any. Test it for yourself. Start with the gullets a little above the surface of the workpiece and make a cut. Then raise the blade to its full height and cut again. Compare the two cuts and decide which is better.

Raising the blade until the gullets clear the top of the workpiece will eliminate overheating and flutter, but the cut might not be the cleanest possible one. The cleanest and most efficient cutting occurs with the blade raised to its maximum height. However, having that much blade exposed above the workpiece might make you nervous.

The correct blade height is somewhere in between. For the cleanest cut, raise the blade; if it rattles you, lower it.

Guard

Every saw cut requires a guard. If you find yourself unable to cover the exposed blade, don't proceed. Find another way to get the job done.

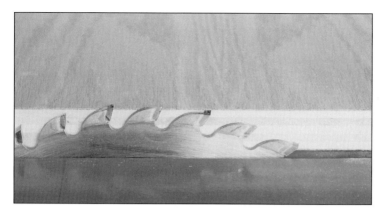

When the blade is low, each tooth spends more time inside the wood, increasing the risk of burning the wood.

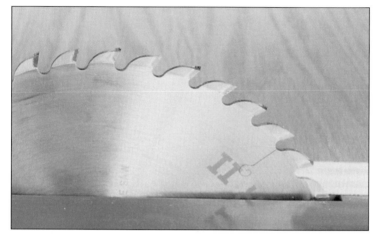

When the blade is high, the cut is at its cleanest and most efficient, but there is a lot of exposed blade, perhaps too much for comfort.

The gullets should clear the top surface of the workpiece. After that, the guarded blade can be as high as the operator finds comfortable.

Operator procedure

Whatever the material and cut, the operator always has the same objective: to complete the operation safely and accurately, and to keep complete control of the machine and the material at all times.

Where to stand

Stand directly in front of the table saw, close to it, but toward the left side of the blade. Starting the cut may oblige you to move back in order to heft the material, but all saw cuts finish in the same way, right at the machine.

Perhaps because of the machine's noise and wind, many people stand too far back, as if behind an invisible barricade. Reaching over this phantom barrier keeps them off balance, unable to manage the workpiece.

Locate yourself by touching the base of the saw, or its leg, with your left foot. This habit allows you to get back into the same place every time, and it positions your body off the line of the cut, out of the way of kickback.

Allow your hip or midriff to contact the edge of the saw table. This helps anchor your body and keep your balance while you work.

Stand with your left foot touching the base of the saw, and with your hip in contact with the machine table.

Where to look

When you're working at the table saw, you need to keep your eyes moving among a number of critical points. Initially, you might think that you have to look at the cut, but that tells you the least. The cut will proceed as long as you keep pushing the wood. It will be right without your looking at it, provided that you keep checking to be sure that the wood is in tight contact with the fence, that the path is clear after the cut, that the wood isn't distorting after the cut, that you are ready to pick up the push sticks as you approach the end of the cut.

Pay the most attention to how the workpiece contacts the fence just ahead of where it starts to cut. Gravity will mostly take care of keeping the wood down on the saw table, but contact between the face edge and the fence is entirely up to the operator.

Glance at the cutting edge and glance at the splitter to be sure the wood is passing freely past it. Keep your eyes moving over the entire sawing operation, but concentrate on the area of contact between the workpiece and the fence.

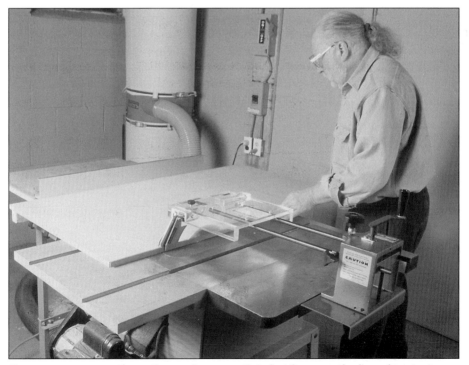

Rove your eyes over the entire sawing operation, but focus on the line of contact between the workpiece and the fence.

Managing the cut

An experienced table saw operator feeds each piece of wood through and past the saw blade in a single smooth movement. In fact, that movement has four distinct stages:

assessing the wood,

entering the wood,

propelling the wood,

ending the cut.

You have to pay attention to different things at each stage. The specifics depend on what you are sawing, so I'll return to these headings later on.

Assessing the wood

As you pick up each piece of wood, look closely at it, both sides. Look for defects that could affect the cut (page 66), and for face side and edge marks (page 64). Then plant either the face side or the face edge down on the saw table, with the other reference surface toward the fence or miter gauge. If the wood hasn't been prepared with a face side or edge, look for flatness, and for one reasonably straight edge.

Entering the wood

Always make sure the wood is held firmly down on the saw table and tight against the fence before you move it into the saw blade. Start the cut gently. The teeth don't appreciate wood being jammed into them.

Any cut made with the blade just kissing the wood is not likely to be accurate. There has to be a falling board of some thickness, even if it's only 1/8 inch. Otherwise, the stresses on the blade are not uniform, disrupting its vertical stance.

Propelling the wood

Once the saw blade enters the wood, you should speed up the cut, especially in dense woods like oak, maple and cherry. With a sharp carbide-tipped blade, you can't feed too quickly. The correct feed speed is the fastest speed that leaves you in full control of the wood. If you feed the wood too slowly, you'll scorch it.

Pay attention to the contact between the wood and the fence, as well as to the cut itself.

Ending the cut

As the cut ends, instead of propelling one piece of wood, you're suddenly dealing with two of them. You have to push the workpiece beyond the blade, while you move the falling board away from the blade. Deal first with the workpiece — the falling board isn't going anywhere for the moment. Push the workpiece completely beyond the blade and splitter. Once the workpiece is clear, withdraw your propelling hand and turn your attention to the falling board. Move it directly toward the left side of the blade, before you attempt to pull it back or lift it off the saw table.

Use a push stick at the end of the cut whenever the workpiece is less than 12 inches wide. Also use a push stick whenever the falling board is narrower than 6 inches.

Using push sticks

Saw guards represent a kind of insurance against injury, but your working defense is to keep your hands 6 to 9 inches away from the saw blade. Doing so means you will need to make and use a pair of push sticks. For more on how to make them, see page 49.

A push stick is an extension of your hand. It allows you to push the work and to hold it down at the same time. You can

At the end of the cut, hold the falling board still with the left push stick while you propel the workpiece entirely past the blade with the right push stick.

With the workpiece clear, withdraw your right hand and use the left push stick to move the falling board away from the blade to the side.

acquire basic skill with push sticks by practicing with the saw turned off. Cut a piece of wood 3 inches wide by 30 inches long, and set the fence about 3-1/2 inches from the blade. With a push stick in each hand, move the wood across the saw table. Flip it up on end, turn it end for end, turn it over and back. Turn the wood so its face edge is against the fence and push it past the blade, then bring it back and turn the face edge to the fence and do it again.

You should always have a pair of push sticks ready to use on the saw table, one on the right and the other on the left. Whenever you feel the urge to touch a piece of scrap that's anywhere near the saw blade, train yourself to pick up a push stick instead. I'll discuss precisely how to use your push sticks in different sawing situations in the next couple of chapters.

Helpers

When you are managing large pieces of wood, or sheets of plywood, you might enlist a helper. It's important that you show your helper exactly where to stand, what to do, and what not to do, before you power up the saw.

The operator must always keep control of the workpiece. The helper's job is to support the workpiece and the falling board. The helper must not attempt to steer, propel or direct the wood in any way. He must hold it up so it remains flat on the saw table, without pulling or pushing on it. If the helper starts to move the workpiece, the operator won't know what is happening. The ensuing confusion invites an accident.

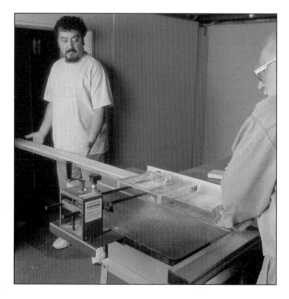

After the cut, if you want the helper to carry the workpiece or the falling board away from the saw, show him exactly when to take control of it, and where to put it.

The helper's job is to support the workpiece and falling board, without pulling or pushing on it.

Some keys to accuracy

Although achieving accuracy is addressed throughout this book, there are a couple of general points to make here. These points may seem obvious to you, but that's why they're not usually mentioned and liable to be ignored.

Prepare the wood with a face side and edge. You cannot do accurate work without these reference surfaces.

For each change in setup, switch the saw off and measure the distance between blade and fence or stop block. Fiddle with the adjustment until it is as close to dead-on as you can make it.

When you're getting out the wood for a project, make some extra stock of each thickness. Use this extra to set up and check your cuts, before you commit the wood itself.

When it's possible to use a stop block, do so. It's always more accurate to index each workpiece against a stop block, instead of trying to cut to a mark on the wood.

Make the saw blade square to the saw table and leave it there. Since the tilting arbor mechanism doesn't work very well, don't use it. Achieve the same results with jigs.

Use jigs and fixtures to stabilize the workpiece and carry it past the saw blade. Clamping the workpiece to a jig is always better than hand-holding it.

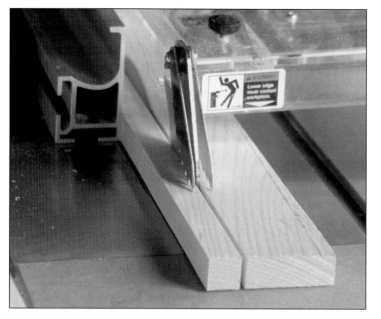

Setup for ripping: The short fence and splitter help prevent kickback.

CHAPTER 7

Ripping Solid Wood

To **rip** means to saw solid wood lengthwise, with the grain. Ripping makes narrower pieces of wood out of wider ones. It's what table saws did first and what they do best.

The diameter of the saw blade determines the thickness that can be ripped. A 10-inch contractor saw projects just over 3 inches from the table, so it cannot rip wood thicker than 3 inches in one pass. There is no practical limit on the length of wood that a standard table saw can rip, and its fence can be opened far enough to accommodate almost any width of board.

Before the table saw can rip, the wood must have a face side and a face edge. Since one edge of the wood bears against the fence during the cut, it must be a straight edge. The newly sawn edge of the wood will be parallel to the fence.

Most ripping is done with the blade at 90 degrees, or square, to the saw table. The newly sawn edge of the wood is square to the face that was in contact with the table during the cut.

Bevels are rip cuts with the saw blade at angles other than 90 degrees. They require tilting the saw's arbor. The ability to tilt the arbor, though marketed as a feature, is one source of inaccuracy in low-price saws. The accurate, easier and safer alternative is a suitable jig (page 132).

Taper sawing is a special case of ripping that requires fastening the wood to a special fixture (page 130).

Deep sawing is another special case of ripping in which you saw half-way through the wood, then turn it over and saw it again (page 86). Deep sawing divides a thick board into two thinner ones. You can deep saw twice the maximum height of the blade, or about 6 inches.

Setup for ripping

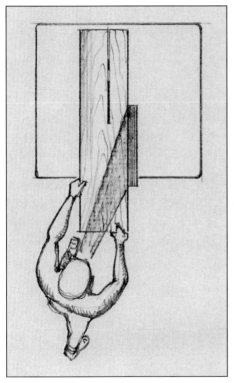

It is dangerous to rip solid wood with a fence that extends all the way across the saw table. If the wood were to distort as it was being cut, it would bind between the blade and fence, throwing the workpiece out of contact with the fence and possibly kicking back.

When ripping, the fence should extend from the front edge of the saw table no farther than the back of the saw blade. To convert a non-adjustable full-length fence for ripping, make a wooden auxiliary fence and fasten it to the regular fence.

Make the auxiliary fence out of hard wood such as maple or cherry, or else from particle board faced with plastic laminate. In height, the auxiliary fence should be about 1/2 inch higher than the saw blade at maximum elevation. It should have a small chip-clearance rebate along its bottom edge. A rebate measuring 1/8 inch by 1/8 inch will be plenty.

Since the auxiliary fence should be easy to mount and remove, attach it to the regular fence with countersunk bolts and wing nuts.

Making the rip cut

Entering the wood

Pick up the workpiece in both hands. The right hand is going to propel the wood into the saw, while the left hand is going to hold it against the fence and down on the table. Whether you are right-handed or left-handed, always stand to the left of the saw blade. This gives you a good view of the cut, allows you to propel the wood easily while maintaining tight contact with the fence, and keeps your body out of the line of kickback.

Start the rip cut with the wood flat on the saw table, or with the trailing end lifted slightly.

Don't lift the leading edge of the wood. The blade will catch it and slam it down hard.

Start the rip cut with the face edge of the board tight against the fence, and with its trailing end up in the air. You want the leading end of the wood to be on the saw table at the start of the cut. It is very dangerous to start the cut with the leading end levered above the surface of the table, because the blade will grab it and slam it down onto the table. Make sure this doesn't happen by lifting the trailing end.

Propelling the wood

Push the workpiece forward with your right hand, while keeping it against the fence with your left hand. Keep your right hand and forearm in line with the wood. Maintain forward movement without stopping. If you pause, you'll cause a score mark on the wood. It is better to feed the wood as quickly as you can while retaining full control. Feeding too slowly allows the saw teeth to rub on the wood and scorch it. Feeding too quickly stalls the motor, which you will hear.

Once the cut has begun, propel the wood smoothly without pausing.

Ending the cut

When the trailing end of the workpiece reaches the saw table, let go with your right hand and pick up the push stick. Position the push stick on the workpiece and resume propelling it forward. Maintain some forward motion with your left hand while you pick up the push stick. Once the right-hand push stick is working, let go with your left hand and pick up the second push stick.

As the tail of the workpiece approaches the saw blade, swing your left hand forward so the push stick continues to press the uncut wood against the saw fence. When you get down to the last inch of wood, place the left push stick right on the corner of the workpiece, or bring it around to the trailing end. Either way, push the workpiece entirely beyond the blade and onto the rear auxiliary table, support rollers, or floor. Guard or no, do not attempt to reach over the saw blade to retrieve the workpiece. When you want to retrieve it, walk around the saw.

As the blade severs the wood, the falling board leaves the workpiece and stops moving. Use the left push stick to move it toward the left side of the saw table, away from the blade. The splitter will keep it from contacting the back edge of the saw blade. Once the falling board is well away from the saw blade, you can lift it farther to the left and off the saw table.

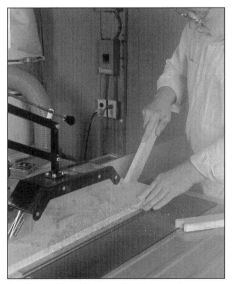 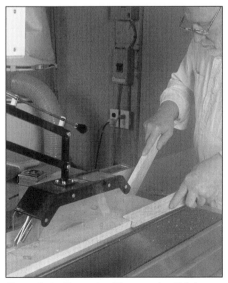

Pick up the right push stick *as the trailing end of the wood moves onto the saw table.*

Complete the cut *with a push stick in each hand.*

Troubleshooting

At the end of a rip cut you want to see a straight, flat surface that is square to the face side and parallel to the face edge. Check it for straightness with your 24-inch straight edge.

Measure the width of the board.

Check it for squareness with the square. Be sure you place the stock of the square against the face of the wood that was down on the saw table — it's meaningless to check for square from the opposite face. Make the check near both ends of the board.

Examine the cut surface to assess its smoothness. A sharp carbide blade and a correctly aligned saw should not leave visible sawing marks. The wood won't be as smooth as a plane could get it, but it will be smooth enough to glue.

It's not straight. Examine both the workpiece and the falling board for distortion. You'll almost certainly find that the wood distorted as it was being cut, not that the saw somehow made a curved shape.

It's not square. Tilt the blade until the cut is square and try again. However, if the amount that the wood is off square changes a lot from one end of the board to the other, see whether the wood hasn't twisted.

It's the wrong width. If the workpiece is consistently the wrong width, from one end to the other, you didn't set the fence in the right place.

It tapers from end to end. The face edge must not have been in contact with the fence for part of its journey. Perhaps there was a piece of sawdust or debris in the way.

The edge is scorched. Scorched wood is almost always a result of feeding too slowly. However, if you speed up and the scorching doesn't improve or gets worse, then the blade is either dirty or dull. Clean it and see if that helps.

Burns indicate feeding too slowly or a dull blade, or both. Score marks show where the sawyer paused in the middle of the cut.

There's a regular pattern of score marks and a ragged edge on the workpiece, or the falling board, or both. The saw blade and fence are not parallel. The marks result from the cut face just brushing the back teeth of the saw. See page 00.

There's a single score mark, or a scorch, about a foot from the trailing end of the board. You paused while picking up the push sticks. With the saw turned off, practice maintaining some amount of forward motion while you change from hand propulsion to push sticks.

Ripping in special situations

Ripping multiples

In general woodworking and home repair, you're as likely to want a dozen pieces the same width. Sawing the wood becomes a problem in managing materials and workflow. Here's how to proceed:

Before you switch on the saw, stack all the wood on the saw table to the right of the fence.

Set up an outfeed table, to catch the wood at the end of each cut. It can be level with the saw table, or a few inches lower, and it can be as simple as plywood on saw horses.

Saw the first piece of wood and check that it is the width you want.

Saw all the wood. Let each workpiece fall onto your outfeed table. Use the push stick to move the scrap away from the saw blade and onto the floor. The saw table itself should be completely clear at the start of each cut.

Pile the newly cut parts to the right of the saw fence. This falling board is wide enough for two or three more workpieces.

Ripping long boards

There's no practical limit on the length of board you can rip, but you must set up outfeed support at the height of the saw table, or very slightly lower. If the outfeed support is higher than the saw table, the wood will hang up. The support can be a saw horse or a roller stand. It should be freestanding so you can move it as necessary.

Do a dry run with the long board to make sure it rides onto the outfeed support. If the wood droops after it leaves the saw table, it might hang up on the outfeed support. Lower the support so this does not happen.

When you enter a long board, you must make sure the leading edge is down tight on the saw table. Stand to the left of the blade and as far back from the saw table as necessary to balance and support the board. Once you have begun the cut, lower the board so it rests flat on the saw table, and feed it by walking forward until your body touches the machine, in the normal position for ripping. Then feed the board as you normally would.

Set up a roller stand or a sawhorse to catch the long board.

To rip a long board, stand as far back as necessary. Make sure the leading end is down on the table.

Ripping thin boards

Two problems may arise when you rip thin wood. First, the wood is liable to droop as it leaves the saw table. The remedy is to set up an outfeed table to support it. Second, very thin material can slip underneath a standard saw fence, or catch in the fence's chip-clearance rebate. The remedy is to fit an auxiliary fence that is tight to the saw table, so the material can't slip under it.

Resawing

Resawing is ripping multiple pieces off a thick or wide board. You would do this to make the stock for splines or for a bent lamination. The wood has to start with a good face side and face edge. Since you want all the pieces the same thickness, set the fence to that thickness, and make a narrow push stick. In this situation the falling board is larger than the workpiece until the very last cut, but nevertheless it's the workpiece you must propel past the saw blade. The splitter is essential when resawing.

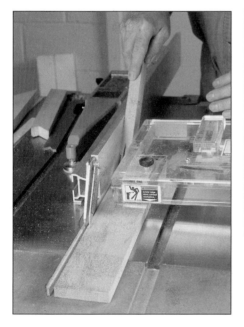

Resawing means ripping multiple strips off a thick or wide board. Make a thin push stick, or expect the regular one to get chewed up. Complete the cut with a push stick in each hand.

Deep sawing

Deep sawing is ripping to split a wide, thick board into two thinner boards. You deep-saw from both edges of the wood, so it's possible to split a board that's twice as wide as the saw's maximum blade height. The first cut is a shaping operation, made with a full length fence. For the second cut, set the fence short as for ripping solid wood. Keep push sticks close at hand for the end of the cut. If your splitter has anti-kickback pawls, you'll have to remove it to deep saw. Leave the guard in place above the workpiece, as a visible reminder of exactly where the blade is cutting.

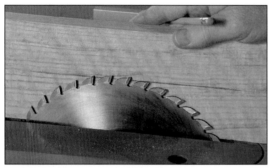

Deep sawing splits a wide and thick board into two thinner ones. You can deep saw almost twice the maximum height of the saw blade.

The splitter with antikickback pawls cannot be used for deep sawing.

To make the second cut, insert a wooden wedge to keep the wood from pinching the blade.

Know where the blade will exit, and complete deep sawing with two push sticks.

Expect some burning when you deep saw a hard wood like this white oak.

Bevels: ripping at angles other than 90 degrees

Bevel sawing means to rip the long edge of the wood to an angle other than 90 degrees. This commonly arises in two situations: bevel-sawing at an angle of 45 degrees, to make a long-grain miter joint, and bevel-sawing at about 15 degrees, to make a traditional raised-and-fielded panel.

As discussed on page 31, although the contractor-style saw has a tilting arbor, it rarely returns to square after being tilted. Therefore you can re-adjust the mechanism after bevel-sawing, or else you can make a jig to hold the wood at the desired angle. Of these two approaches, I recommend keeping the blade at 90 degrees to the table and making suitable jigs (page 132). Unusual angles may be necessary for making wooden hoppers, barrels or staved columns, but it's quick to make a simple jig for each new situation. Clamping the wood to the jig is much more accurate than sliding it freehand along the fence and saw table.

If you do tilt the arbor, always set up the cut so the fence remains on the right side of the blade. If you were to move the fence to the left side, you would trap the workpiece between the fence and blade, inviting it to kick back.

The table saw does an excellent job of beveling the edge of raised-and-fielded panels. It requires a suitable jig, as discussed on page 134.

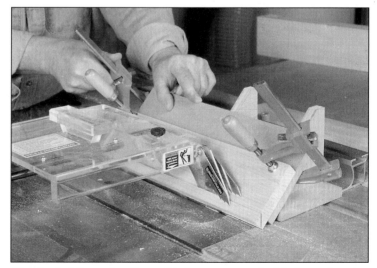

Simple sled jig makes it possible to saw accurate 45-degree bevels. Page 132.

Ripping difficult wood

At the breakdown stage, it's important to examine all the wood before you turn the saw on. You may find some pieces that are not safe to rip. Mark the problems with crayon or chalk, and set these boards aside for special handling. Look for these conditions:

Twist. It's neither safe nor accurate to rip twisted boards. The wood cannot maintain solid contact with the table or the fence. It will move into the blade in unpredictable ways. The remedy is to crosscut twisted pieces into short lengths, thereby reducing the effect of the twist.

Cup. You can rip cupped wood. Put the hollow side up and rip down the center of the board. Make sure the center line remains in touch with the table as the cut proceeds.

Crook. Crooked wood can't be ripped safely. No matter which way you orient it, it will bind between the fence and blade. The remedy is either to crosscut it into short pieces, or to fasten it to a straight plank and straighten one edge, same as a waney-edge board.

Bow. Rip bowed wood with the hollow side of the bow uppermost. This allows you to feed the wood into the blade with the leading end down tight on the saw table, and to steer so the portion being cut is always flat on the table. If you cut it the other way up, the descending teeth will slam the wood down onto the saw table.

Knots. Make sure there are no loose knots. If there are any, knock them out. If you saw into a knot that is near the edge of the wood, the falling board is likely to break free at the knot, jamming the saw or flying through the air.

Waney edge. A board with two waney edges can't be sawn because there is no straight edge to guide against the saw fence. The remedy is to fasten a guide board on top of the workpiece. The guide board can be any straight piece that's as long as the workpiece, or longer. Fasten it to the workpiece with nails or screws, so it overhangs the edge. The sawn edge will be the opposite edge of the workpiece, so the guide board should be parallel to the cut you want. You can make sure of it by snapping chalk lines on the workpiece, and measuring back to the edge of the guide board.

Ripping waney edged wood with a guide board

Snap a chalk line to locate the cut on the waney-edged board.

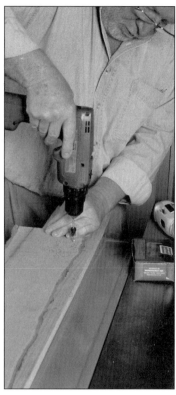

Screw through the waste to fasten the waney board to a straight guide board. Make it parallel to the chalk line.

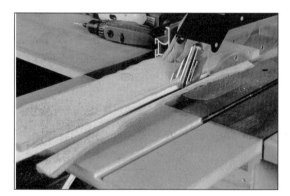

Saw the first edge with the guide board running against the fence.

Remove the guide board and saw the second edge in the usual manner.

You can saw half-sheets of plywood on the contractor's saw, but full sheets should be broken down by some other method.

CHAPTER 8

Sawing Sheet Materials

Man-made sheet materials include plywoods of various types and thicknesses, particle boards, and fiberboards. From a sawing perspective, sheet materials differ from solid wood in two important ways:

Except for the structurally unimportant face veneers on plywood, there's **no grain direction**;

They are **dimensionally stable.**

As a consequence of these two differences, sheet materials do not distort during the cut. Although the face veneer on plywood does not affect how you set up the saw, when sawing across its grain there may be some rag-out on the bottom side. Carbide-tipped blades minimize the amount of ragging out, and you can further minimize it by sawing with the best veneer uppermost.

The problem when sawing man-made boards is the size of the sheet. While it's possible to feed a full 4x8 sheet across the top of a contractor's-style table saw, it's not advisable unless you have built your saw into the middle of a sea of extension tables. The alternative is to break the sheet down into manageable pieces using a handsaw, a jigsaw, or a portable circular saw.

Once you get the sheet small enough to manage comfortably on your setup, always keeping it flat on the saw table and maintaining good contact with the fence, you can saw it.

Setup for sheet materials

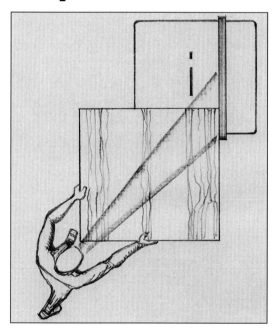

Always use the splitter and use the guard to saw sheet materials. The splitter keeps the workpiece and falling board from contacting the back edge of the blade, thereby preventing kickback. The top guard keeps your hands out of the saw blade.

As discussed on page 38, some styles of guard are more suitable for sawing large sheets. If you do as I do, and break down the sheet before sawing it into accurately dimensioned parts, you'll be able to use a right-mounted or left-mounted guard. However, if you saw a lot of sheet goods and build your saw into the center of a large extension table, you'll need either a right-mounted overarm guard, or a ceiling-mounted guard.

As with solid wood, use push sticks whenever the sawing operation would bring your hand closer than 9 inches to the saw blade. With sheet materials, you're often sawing a workpiece of 12 inches or wider, and leaving a falling board of the same size. In that situation you don't need push sticks.

Saw fence and miter gauge

Since man-made sheet materials don't distort while they're being sawn, you can use a full-length fence. The fence should extend right across the saw table, parallel to the face of the saw blade, and it should sit down tight on the table. If the fence has any tendency to wag at the outfeed end, block it with a board clamped to the table.

Use the miter gauge when you want to make a square end on long sheet materials that are less than 12 inches wide.

Blade height

Raise the saw blade so the gullets clear the top of the sheet. You'll get the cleanest cut with the blade raised to its maximum height, so the teeth spend the minimum time inside the wood. A high blade makes a breeze and it's inhibiting. Set the height somewhere in between clearing the gullets and maximum, but exactly where depends on your comfort.

Extension tables

If you're supporting the sheet on the infeed side, what happens to it at the end of the cut? You can't slide the workpiece back between the fence and the blade. A fall to the floor is certain to ding the corners. Before you begin, set up extension tables on the outfeed side, and possibly on the left side as well, to support the workpiece and the falling board at the end of the cut.

If the saw fence wags at the outfeed side, block it in place by clamping a board to the saw table.

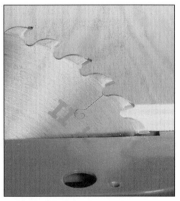

A high blade makes the cleanest cut in sheet materials. Saw with the face veneer upward.

Operator procedure

Your initial stance depends on the size of sheet you are sawing. Stand far enough away to the left of the blade to get your right hand on the trailing edge of the sheet, with your left hand on its left edge. The right hand propels the sheet through the saw, while the left hand presses it toward the saw fence. Both hands support the sheet so it remains flat on the saw table.

Walk the workpiece through the saw. Glance at the cut itself, but keep your attention on the line of contact between workpiece and fence.

To start the cut, support the sheet so its leading edge is tight on the saw table and the guide edge is tight to the saw fence.

Remain standing at the left corner of the saw table as you propel the sheet along the fence.

Propelling the workpiece

As with solid wood, enter the cut slowly. Once you've started the cut, speed up and complete it without pause or hesitation. If you feed too slowly, you'll burn the wood, and if you pause, you'll create a saw mark. You can't feed too quickly, as long as you remain in control of the workpiece.

Ending the cut

Once the saw severs the material, the operator pushes both workpiece and falling board past the blade and onto an outfeed table or into the hands of a helper. You can't draw the workpiece back between the blade and fence, because of the antikickback pawls, and even without them you would be liable to rub against the spinning blade or get crosswise with it, with bad results. Walk around the machine and collect the material. If you can draw the falling board away to the left of the saw blade, you can slide it back.

If you enlist a helper, make sure he knows what to do, and what not to do (page 76). The helper's job is to take control of both workpiece and falling board once you have pushed them past the saw blade. He takes them off the saw table and sets them to one side. However, during the cut, the helper must do nothing more than support the material. He must not attempt to pull it or steer it in any way. That's the sawyer's job, and any interference is asking for trouble.

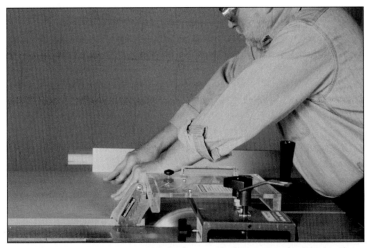

Push the workpiece past the blade, then walk around the saw to lift the sheet and reposition it for the next cut.

Troubleshooting

After sawing man-made sheet materials, you should expect to see straight and clean edges that are square to the surface as well as to one another. There should be no saw marks, scorched wood, or torn face veneer.

The edge isn't straight. You lost contact with the fence during the cut. As a result, the workpiece probably is too small.

The face veneer is torn and ragged across the cut. If the face veneer was down on the saw table, turn the wood over so it is on top. Raise the blade as high as you can. Use a blade with more teeth. Be sure the blade is sharp. Lay a strip of masking tape on the line of cut, on the board's underside.

I did all of the above and the cut still rags. This is a difficult problem to diagnose. The fence has to be dead parallel to the blade, with no tolerance for error. The most common cause is the back edge of the blade brushing the work, but the rag could instead be coming from the front edge. To find out, cut about 2 inches into a spare piece of the same material. Stop the saw and let it run down. Now look at the cut. If it rags, adjust the infeed end of the fence. If there's no rag, adjust the outfeed end.

The sawn edge is scorched. You were feeding too slowly.

The piece is the wrong size. Check your setup. Don't try to trim a piece by skimming it with the saw blade. If there is no falling board, the blade is operating in an unbalanced condition and it will not make a true cut.

There's a score mark midway along the edge. You probably paused in the middle of the cut. Make the cut in one continuous motion, without pausing or stopping.

A skimming cut, without a falling board, probably will not be accurate, because the work stress falls on only one side of the blade.

Special situations with sheet materials

Fence or miter gauge?

Once you have one square end, you can make many cuts using the fence, as long as the short side of the workpiece exceeds 12 inches. Change to the miter gauge or crosscut box when the material gets small and any time the proposed cut creates a workpiece longer than it is wide. The danger you're trying to avoid is being unable to keep the end of the workpiece tight against the fence, so it pivots diagonally and jams. Assess the risk with the power off and the blade lowered below the table. Rehearse the cut, and see how it feels.

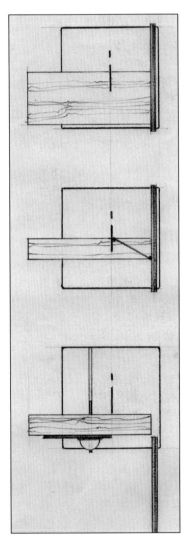

Change point. When the fence-guided edge is less than 12 inches long, switch to the miter gauge.

***VERY DANGEROUS.** The wood is liable to pivot on the diagonal, become trapped, and jam or fly.*

A sliding fence can be moved back and used as a stop block. The workpiece must be clear of the fence before it contacts the blade.

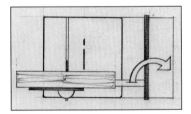

With a fixed fence, *move it to the right and use a square-ended stop block to position the workpiece. Lift the block away before you begin each cut.*

Factory edge

Sheet materials come with reasonably straight manufactured edges. However, they are not perfect, and for accurate work you'll want to saw them off. Similarly, while the corner of the sheet is likely to be square, there's no guarantee. You've got to check it, and you'll probably want to saw it square yourself.

In most situations, you'll have broken down the sheet with a handsaw or portable power saw. That sawn edge is even less accurate than the manufactured one. The following procedure straightens the edges of sheet materials. Expect to lose 1/4 inch of wood to each cut. This means you need to start with 3/4 inch of extra width to finish with accurate dimensions.

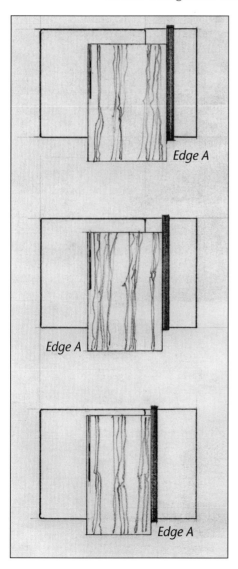

Edge A

Edge A

Edge A

First cut. Run the manufactured edge, or the best sawn edge (A in the drawings), against the fence to saw off the opposite edge. Saw just far enough into the sheet to create a falling board — a thin wafer of 1/16 inch is enough. If you were to just kiss the edge of the sheet with the saw blade, you would not get an accurate cut.

Second cut. Reset the fence and run the newly sawn edge against the fence to saw off the first guide edge. As before, saw just far enough into the sheet to create a falling board.

Dimensioning cuts. Now you can saw the sheet into smaller pieces, guiding either of the newly sawn edges against the fence or miter gauge.

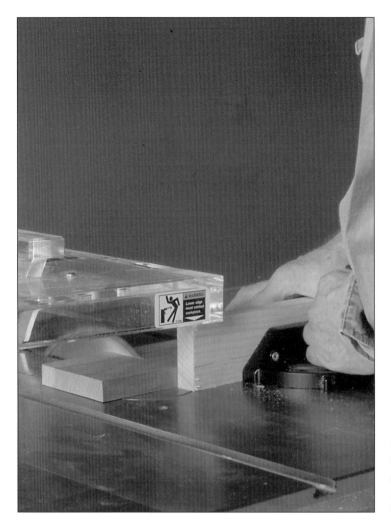

Crosscut with a wooden auxiliary fence screwed to the miter gauge.

CHAPTER 9

Crosscutting

We use the table saw to crosscut solid wood for two reasons:

to make one end of the wood square;

to make the second end square and to length.

At best, the end-grain surface created by a carbide-tipped blade is superb, and can't be improved with any other tool. Consequently there is no reason not to crosscut to finished length.

Crosscutting is fundamentally different from ripping for two reasons. First, crosscuts are by definition made across the long grain of the wood, not with it. Second, the wood is always held tightly against the fence of the miter gauge, it never travels independently. The gauge and the wood always move together toward the saw blade. This means you can clamp the wood to the gauge, which is one important technique toward achieving accuracy.

Crosscutting to length normally is a two-step operation. First, cut one end of the wood square. Second, fit a stop block to the fence on the crosscut gauge and cut the second end square and to length. The stop block is always more accurate than crosscutting to a mark on the wood.

Crosscuts at angles other than 90 degrees are called miters, with the most common miter cut being at 45 degrees. It's rare, but once in a while a crosscut or miter has to be made with the blade tilted to some angle other than 90 degrees. This is called a compound miter.

All of these cuts can be made with the aid of the saw's miter gauge, or with a shop-built crosscut box. The gauge or box mounts into the guide slots that are milled into the table. The gauge or box holds the work while you push it past the saw blade.

The shop-made crosscut box is a good alternative to the miter gauge. Page 136.

Setup for crosscutting

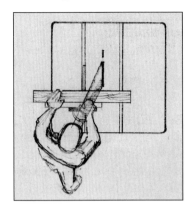

Guarding the blade for crosscutting may affect which side of the blade the workpiece traverses, and may also affect where the operator stands. There are two guide slots in the saw table, and you can use the one that gives you the more comfortable control of workpiece and falling board.

As with any table saw operation, it's important to establish contact between the machine and your body. Stand where you can get a clear view of the cut, without standing directly in line with the blade.

Right-mounted overarm guard. Run the miter gauge in the left-hand table slot, with the workpiece to the left of the saw blade. This allows you to stand in the normal operator position, to the left of the saw blade, with your foot touching the saw base, or your mid-section touching the saw table.

Left-mounted overarm guard. Run the miter gauge in the right-hand table slot, with the workpiece extending to the right of the saw blade. The operator must move to the right side of the saw blade, with one foot touching the right leg of the saw stand.

Standard guard. The standard metal guard that comes with most saws rides up when the wood contacts it. Before you make a cut, be sure the auxiliary fence passes under the guard. Run the miter gauge in the left-hand table slot and stand in the normal position, to the left of the saw blade.

With a left-mounted saw guard, run the crosscut gauge in the right-hand table slot. Raise the guard high enough to clear the auxiliary fence.

Splitter

Do not remove the splitter when using the miter gauge. It will help keep the falling board from coming into contact with the back edge of the saw blade. It's normally removed when working with a crosscut box.

Miter gauge and auxiliary fence

To make a square crosscut, set the miter gauge to 90 degrees. It sounds stupidly obvious, but the obvious often is the factor we're quick to ignore. To check that the miter gauge is square to its bar, saw a piece of wood and check it with your square. When the gauge produces a square piece of wood, it is set at 90 degrees, no matter what its pointer suggests.

Miter gauges have screw holes for attaching a wooden auxiliary fence, which you should always do. The auxiliary crosscut fence should be:

At least **an inch thick**. The thick fence ensures adequate support for thin stock under the stress of sawing.

Higher than the thickness of the wood you intend to saw.

About **16 inches long**.

Screw the fence to the miter gauge, then move it through the saw to cut off one end. The sawn end now serves as an accurate indicator of where the saw will cut. The other end of the fence can extend as far as convenient — far enough for a stop block. As with push sticks, don't make a precious fence, because it will get chewed up. Instead, make a new fence for each new crosscutting situation.

Screw the auxiliary fence to the miter gauge, then saw one end off.

Stop blocks

Use a stop block when you want to crosscut a number of pieces to the same setting. Saw one end of each piece, then clamp the stop block to the auxiliary fence, check the setting, and saw the other end of all the pieces. Stop blocks produce greater accuracy than crosscutting to a line, no matter how exact your layout marks.

You can buy auxiliary fence attachments with flip-up stop blocks, and two-position stops. Flip-up and two-position stops allow you to saw both ends of a piece of wood while you've got it in your hand. You can make special stop blocks

Saw the first end with the stop block flipped out of the way.

Cut the workpiece to length using the stop block.

Clamp a wooden stop block to the auxiliary fence.

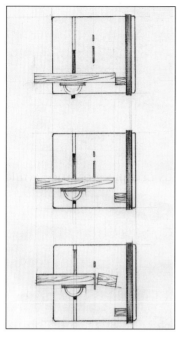

for special situations, such as sawing miters on both ends of a piece of wood (page 109).

It's possible to use the saw's regular rip fence as a stop. First, make a block about 6 inches long with both ends square. Next, slide the miter gauge to within a couple of inches of the near side of the saw table. Then move the fence to where the workpiece and the stop block together butt into the fence. Hold the workpiece on the miter gauge in the usual way and make the cut, leaving the stop block behind. The workpiece must not be touching the stop block when it reaches the saw blade. This procedure ensures that there is plenty of space between the side of the blade and the fence. There has to be enough space for the workpiece to rotate diagonally without getting jammed.

Operator procedure for crosscutting

While you can hand-hold the wood against the auxiliary fence on the miter gauge, you will get the most accurate result if you clamp it there.

Clamping the wood to the miter-gauge fence is not a sign of weakness. You probably do have the strength to hold the wood firmly in position. What no one has is the ability to hold it exactly the same way every time. When you are trying to work as accurately as possible, the difference in muscle tension from one cut to the next is enough to produce two different-sized pieces of wood.

***Entering the cut.** Ease the saw teeth into the wood.*

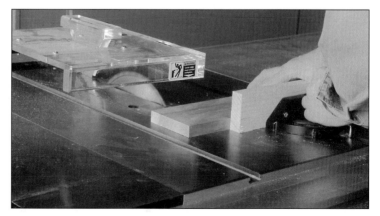

Entering the wood

Always begin the cut slowly, so the saw teeth ease into the wood, then speed up as the cut progresses. If you jam the wood into the saw blade, you may throw the cut off the mark, and you might damage the teeth. This is where hand-held stock moves on the gauge, but clamped stock doesn't.

Propelling the wood

Clamp or not, hold the wood against the fence with both hands. Stand far enough to the side to be sure your wrist and elbow won't move into the blade as the cut progresses. Push the gauge and workpiece into the saw blade with steady, even pressure.

Ending the cut

As soon as the workpiece clears the front of the saw blade, it will be severed into two pieces. If you are hand-holding the workpiece, slide it away from the blade along the fence, then withdraw the gauge back to the starting position. If you have clamped the workpiece to the fence, just pull the gauge straight back.

The problem now is what to do about the falling board. If it catches on the back teeth as they rise out of the saw table, it's liable to be picked up and thrown at you. You have to get it away from the blade without pivoting it into the back edge of the blade.

Propel the miter gauge and workpiece past the front of the saw blade, then withdraw both.

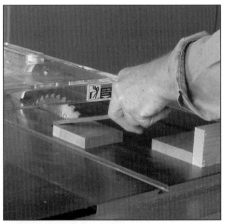

Once the workpiece is clear of the blade, retrieve the falling board with a push stick.

The falling board is easy to remove when it is long enough to protrude out beyond the blade guard. Grab the free end with your hand or with a push stick, and draw it straight sideways, away from the blade, then remove it from the saw table.

The falling board is a problem when it remains covered by the blade guard. You may have no alternative but to shut the saw off and lift the guard in order to flick it away from the blade.

A different problem arises when you are merely trimming the end of the workpiece. The falling board will be a little wafer of wood, and one of three things will happen.

The wind from the blade will blow the wafer away from the blade, no problem.

The wafer will disappear down the space between the blade and table insert, no problem.

The wafer will start down the space between blade and insert, and stick there. The solution is not to saw onward regardless, but to shut off the saw and remove the wafer of wood and consider a new insert with less gap.

Using the crosscut box

The crosscut box has two advantages over the miter gauge. First, by carrying the workpiece, it removes the variable of skidding the wood directly on the surface of the saw table. Second, its fence makes a secure place to clamp stop blocks, and gives you a broad surface to push without getting your hands near the blade. It's a very safe and certain solution to crosscutting. Details of making the crosscut box appear on page 136.

Clamp the workpiece and the stop block to the crosscut box.

Troubleshooting

At the end of the crosscut you want to see a straight, flat surface that is square to the face edge and face side. The newly sawn surface should be clean and smooth, with no saw marks or torn grain.

It's not square. First, verify that you are checking from the face side and edge, or at least from the surfaces that were to the fence and table. Next, see whether there was a bit of debris between the workpiece and the crosscut fence. Third, check the saw setup. Make sure the blade is square to the table. When you're sure of the setup, crosscut the piece again and check the new end. Then assess the deviation and adjust the saw and miter gauge accordingly. Clamp the wood to the crosscut fence and try again.

It's mostly square but one corner heels off. The wood moved during the cut, and you probably felt it happen. Clamp it to the fence on the miter gauge.

It's the wrong length. Either the stop block is in the wrong place, or a speck of crud kept the workpiece from contacting it. Correct the setup, and this time clamp the workpiece to the crosscut fence.

The wood looks scorched. You were feeding too slowly. Enter the wood slowly, but then speed up through the cut.

The bottom and back of the cut are ragged. Try setting the blade at different heights. You may have been feeding too fast. Too slow will burn the wood, but when crosscutting, too fast will cause rag-out. Clean the blade and see whether it's sharp. If you have a new sharp blade, try it and see if the cut improves.

Crosscutting in special situations

As with all table saw operations, you'll encounter special crosscut situations that force you to consider how to proceed safely and accurately, or whether to proceed at all. In many situations, a crosscut box is the best solution. It allows you to clamp the work to a sliding bed, eliminating the variable of friction between workpiece and table.

Long boards

Sawing a long board in half is straightforward, because the wood balances across the saw table. Set up some kind of support on the left side of the saw table so the wood doesn't drop out of control as it's being severed. A table-high saw horse is plenty of support.

Sawing one end off a long board is difficult because the board is out of balance. You can do it with supports and care, but consider whether a table saw is the best tool for the job. Other tools would be a hand saw, a portable circular saw, a chop saw or a portable jig saw. A crosscut box with a support makes almost any length of board more manageable.

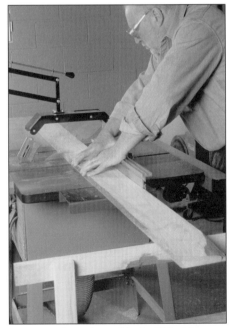

To saw a long board in half, hold or clamp it on the miter gauge and support one end on a sawhorse.

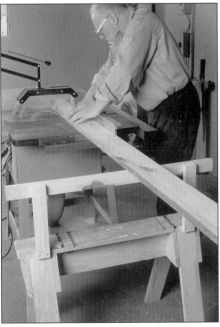

It's more awkward to saw one end off a long board, but the technique is the same.

Wide boards

You rarely get solid wood, any more, that's too wide to cross-cut in the usual way. If you do happen to have such a wide plank, you may need to support it with a pair of table-high saw horses on the infeed side, and perhaps on the outfeed side as well. If you have a lot of wide wood, you can make a crosscut box sized to it.

Small pieces

Make small pieces of wood by sawing them off larger pieces. Trouble arises when you want to saw a little bit off a small piece. When the little piece is longer than about 3 inches, there's enough room to clamp it to the fence on the miter gauge, and it's no problem to saw. When it is smaller than about 3 inches, you won't have room for the clamp, but you don't have much investment in materials either. The remedy is to saw another little piece off the larger piece of wood, and get it the right size this time. Small pieces of wood that are wider than they are long are dangerous to crosscut on the miter gauge, but safe when clamped in the crosscut box.

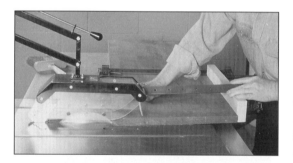

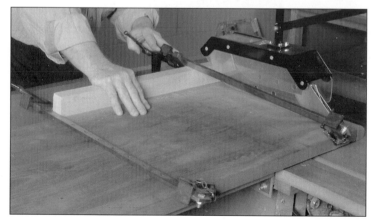

Clamp the wide plank to the auxiliary fence on the miter gauge. You may need to begin the cut with the gauge extended off the saw table.

Miters

Crosscutting a miter is hardly different from sawing a square end. Make a new fence for the miter gauge, and arrange the gauge in the table slots so the high end of the wood enters the cut first. To eliminate movement between the wood and the fence, clamp the two together.

Add auxiliary fences to the crosscut box to adapt it for miter cuts. If you saw a lot of 45-degree miters, make a sliding crosscut box specifically for them.

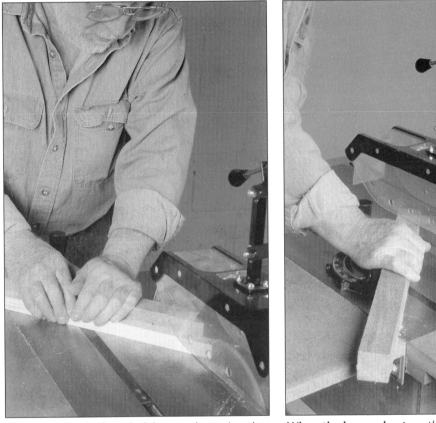

Miter with the high end of the wood entering the cut first. This allows you to keep your hands well back, away from the action.

When the low end enters, the sawyer must reach awkwardly far across the saw table.

Miters on both ends

When you want to miter both ends of a number of parts, the feather edge on the first end won't register accurately against a regular stop block. Begin by mitering one end on all the pieces. Then use the scrap to make a 45-degree stop block. Clamp the stop block to the auxiliary fence. This setup makes a positive, unambiguous stop for the mitered end. It's perhaps the only way to table-saw double-mitered parts that actually are the same length.

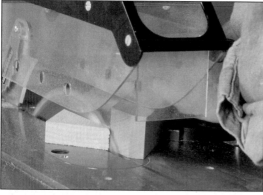

Miter one end of all the parts.

Clamp a 45-degree stop block to the auxiliary fence.

Miter the second end by clamping the workpiece tight against the 45-degree stop block.

Crosscutting difficult wood

When you are breaking parts out of larger pieces of wood, it's important to take a close look at all the wood before crosscutting any of it. You may find some pieces that are not safe to crosscut, or some that should be ripped first. Mark the problems with crayon or chalk, and set these boards aside for special handling. Look for these conditions:

Twist. You can crosscut twisted boards. Anchor the workpiece firmly against the fence with a clamp.

Cup. It's best to rip cupped wood before crosscutting, in order to reduce the cup. But you can crosscut it by clamping the workpiece. Position it whichever way up gives you the best clamping effect.

Crook and wane. You can't crosscut crooked or sprung wood, nor can you crosscut a waney-edged board that has no straight edge. The instant it severs into two pieces, it will lose contact with the fence and go out of control. The remedy is to fasten a guide board onto the crooked board and straighten one edge before crosscutting, as discussed on page 89.

Bow. You can crosscut bowed wood either way up. If the hollow side is up, lift one end so the cut itself occurs in wood that's flat on the table. If the hollow side is down, press the board flat on the saw table.

Knots. Knock loose knots out of the wood. Tight knots don't pose a sawing problem. When you're sawing softwood, the objective generally is to eliminate as many knots as possible by crosscutting them out of the wood.

CHAPTER 10

Shaping Wood

The term "shaping" includes any table saw operation that does not saw the wood into two pieces. The most common shaping operations include:

sawing grooves,

sawing rebates,

sawing housings or dadoes,

making moldings,

raising panels,

making joints.

You can make many shaping cuts with a regular saw blade, using the standard fence and miter gauge or crosscut box. You can also equip the saw with a dado head or with a shaper-type cutterhead that carries profiled knives. These accessories allow you to shape edges and make moldings. The table saw is surprisingly versatile in this regard, performing many of the same operations as a router table or small shaper. Although raising panels and many joint-making operations qualify as shaping, most require making jigs (page 122).

For accurate results, always check your setup with an extra piece of wood. Routinely prepare extra stock in order to have test pieces for checking setups.

Setup for shaping

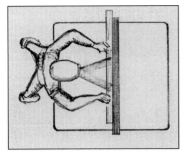

Most shaping operations can be done in more than one way. For example, you can make a rebate with two passes of the saw blade, or with one pass over a dado head. Deciding which way to proceed involves the blades available, the amount of wood that will be removed, the number of passes it will take to remove all of the wood, and the number of pieces you intend to machine. It's always best to minimize the number of passes across the saw blade or cutterhead. Each pass is another chance for things to go wrong.

For accurate results when shaping, the workpiece must be square and regular, preferably with a face side and edge. Any deviation from flat and square will make the cut inaccurate.

Guard and splitter

The saw blade, dado head or molding head must be guarded for all shaping operations. Most overarm guards will do a good job. However, unless the splitter rises and falls with the saw blade, it will interfere and must be removed.

The combined guard-and-splitter that comes as standard equipment on most contractor-type table saws cannot be used for shaping. Replace it with an after-market guard, or else do your shaping with the router or shaper.

Blade height and feed speed

Any ATB or flat-top carbide-tipped saw blade can be used for shaping. The blade height depends on the shape you want to make. For most shaping cuts, the blade is quite low to the saw table. This means the teeth are fully buried in the wood, and feeding too quickly is liable to cause some fluttering that will affect accuracy. Feed at the same rate you would for regular sawing, but focus your attention on the contact between workpiece and fence.

Table insert

You can use the regular table insert for shaping with the saw blade. Dado heads and molding heads, however, require inserts with wide slots, which you can buy or make (page 43).

Fence and miter gauge

For all shaping operations, the fence runs all the way across the saw table. Since tight contact is critical, you're liable to put a considerable amount of pressure against the fence. Most fences will deflect, unless you clamp the free end to the saw table, or anchor it against a clamped block.

Since most shaping cuts are shallow and don't sever the wood, it's safe to use the fence with the miter gauge. A typical situation is sawing a housing across the grain of the wood. The miter gauge carries the workpiece to the cutter, while the fence acts as an end stop to locate the cut. For best results, clamp the wood to the miter gauge.

Operator procedure for shaping

When shaping, stand on the left side of the saw table. This gives you a good view of the contact between the workpiece and fence, and it allows you to press and propel the workpiece.

People tend to stand in front of the saw or on the left corner, but this is a hold-over from sawing the wood instead of shaping it. Some styles of left-mounted overarm guard may interfere with standing fully to the left side, but get as far over as you can.

Stabilize the fence against the pressure of shaping with a block clamped to the saw table.

You'll get the best view and closest control of most shaping operations by standing on the left side of the saw table.

Sawing grooves

We generally saw grooves to make spline joints and to retain a glass or plywood panel. Grooves run with the grain direction of the workpiece. Cross-grain grooves are called dadoes, or housings (page 118). The simplest groove is one pass along the fence and over the saw blade, making a groove 1/8 inch wide. To saw wider grooves, make the two outer cuts first, then make multiple cuts to remove the waste from the middle. It won't take many multiple cuts to persuade you to use a dado head instead of the regular saw blade.

Since the dial caliper has a pair of spurs for inside measurement, it's perfect for checking the dimensions of grooves.

For accuracy, saw grooves with the face edge and face side of the workpiece against the saw table and fence. In furniture making, this orientation comes automatically from the practice of putting the face edge toward the back and the face side toward the inside.

While you can make grooves with multiple passes of the regular saw blade, it's quicker and more accurate to install the dado head.

A housing or dado is a groove made across the grain of the workpiece.

Make grooves with the guard tight to the workpiece, leaving room for your push stick.

Sawing rebates

A rebate is a square cut-out along the corner of the wood. Small rebates, up to about 1/4 inch on a side, generally are made for decoration. Larger rebates, typically up to 3/4 inch on a side, generally make a joint, hold glass, or retain a panel. Square rebates can be sawn with two passes on a single setup. Unequal rebates will need two setups. Any rebate can be cut with a single pass over a dado head, and when there are more than a few to make, this is the better way to go. It's quicker, and more accurate.

Small decorative rebate can be sawn all around a piece of wood.

An equal rebate should be sawn with the rebate falling between the blade and fence. If you try it the other way, with the bulk of the workpiece between blade and fence, it will require two setups instead of one. It doesn't matter whether you make the saw cut in the face of the wood first, or the one in the edge.

Make the first cut with the workpiece pressed tight against the fence.

Keep the guard in place as you extend the rebate around the workpiece.

Since the workpiece was up on edge for the first cut, it has to be face down for the second cut.

A rebate is one of the few sawing operations that must be set up by measuring from the fence to the left side of the saw teeth. The most common setup error is measuring as if for ripping, to the right edge of the blade.

Rebating the end of the workpiece introduces a new problem, because one cut has to be made with the workpiece standing up on end. Unless the wood is wider than about 4 inches, this cut is not safe to make using the fence alone. You can stabilize it by clamping the workpiece to a larger piece of wood, or by clamping it to the fence of the crosscut box. The best way to cut an end-rebate, however, is with the tenoning jig (page 139).

Large, unequal rebate allows these two parts to fit together. To make a strong joint, add glue and clamp.

To set up a rebate, measure from the fence to the far side of the saw blade, not the near side as when ripping.

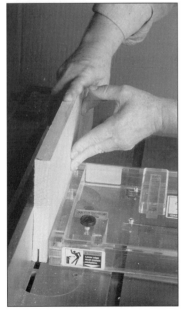

Make the edge cut first.

The second cut frees a small falling board, like the one left of the fence.

Sawing housings

Housings or dadoes are grooves made across the grain of the workpiece. They're often made to partially enclose another piece of wood, like the end of a shelf, hence the name. In wide pieces of wood or sheet materials, you can saw housings by guiding the end of the workpiece against the saw fence. For narrow pieces, carry the workpiece on the miter gauge, with the fence as an end stop. As with wide grooves, it doesn't take a lot of multiple passes before you put the saw blade aside and mount the dado head.

Make repeat housings by clamping a stop block to the crosscut fence.

The dial caliper measures the width of the housing.

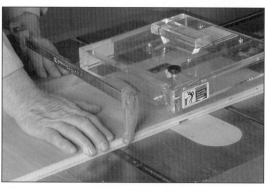

Clamping the workpiece to the crosscut fence also improves stability and accuracy. This cut is the second one in a wide housing.

Troubleshooting: The housing and the rebate are not the same depth. Either the wood wasn't pressed tight against the saw table or fence, or the wood is cupped or twisted.

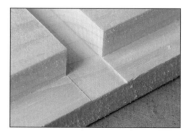

Molding head

Several manufacturers make three-knife molding heads that can be mounted on the table saw arbor. These devices give the saw some of the capability of the shaper. You can use the molding head to profile the faces and edges of furniture parts as well as to run quantities of moldings for carpentry.

When you have a choice between routing a shape and making it on the table saw, choose the saw. Its solid table and fence helps you work accurately. The disadvantage of shaping on the saw is that you give up the ability to saw while the molding head is mounted.

Whatever the precise shape you want to make, there are some general considerations and tactics concerning the setup, fence, and methods of guiding the workpiece.

A three-knife molding head allows you to make many different moldings.

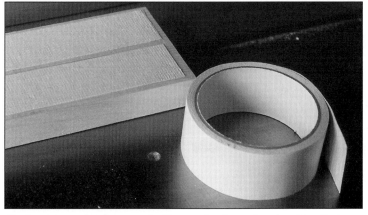

Fasten a wooden fence onto the regular fence for shaping. Fasten it with screws or with double-stick tape. You can raise the molding head into the auxiliary fence without damaging the regular fence.

Fence for moldings

As when shaping with the saw blade, the fence must run all the way across the saw table, and most types need a clamp to anchor the outfeed side. When a shaping operation requires raising the knife into the fence in order to use only part of the profile, make an auxiliary fence and fasten it to the regular one with screws or double-faced tape.

Usually there is a choice whether to shape with the cutter tight to the fence, or with the workpiece traveling between the cutter and the fence. It's always safer to shape with the cutter near the fence, because there's less exposed hazard.

Cutter buried in wooden fence.

If you shape with the workpiece traveling between the cutter and the fence, any error results in an extra-deep cut. There's no recovery from cutting too deep — you'll have to discard that piece and shape another. On the other hand, if you shape with the cutter and fence together, any error results in a shallow cut. You can recover by feeding the workpiece again.

Always leave part of the edge unshaped, so it can bear against the fence or saw table to guide the cut. Shaping operations that remove the whole of the edge are not safe without a split fence or a work-holding jig.

Mold one or both edges of a wide workpiece.

Rip the finished moldings off the wide workpiece.

Hold-downs

The safest way to make small-sectioned moldings, such as shoe molds or panel-retaining strips, is to shape the profile on both edges of a wide board. Then rip the moldings off the board, and shape some more. This strategy can become extremely tedious when the table saw has been set up for shaping, and now must be reconfigured for sawing, then back to shaping.

To get around this, use some combination of fingerboards and hold-downs to guide small-sectioned strips past the molding head. The photo below shows a typical setup. What not to do is attempt to steer small pieces by hand or with push sticks. At best the wood will vibrate and chatter, while at worst it will shatter and be thrown back at you.

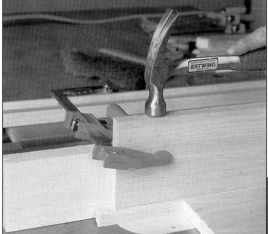

To mold narrow pieces of wood, set up a tight tunnel. The plywood clamped to the saw table holds the workpiece against the fence, and the top board holds it down. Adjust the setup by tapping with a hammer, with the saw turned off.

Feed the workpiece through the tunnel. Complete the cut by pushing a second workpiece behind the first.

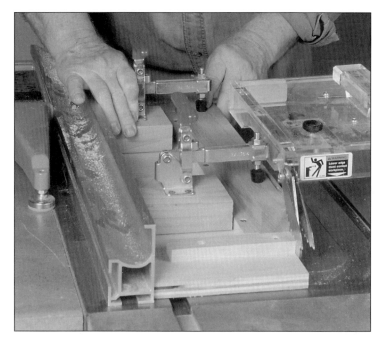

The taper jig is a sled jig with stops and clamps to hold the workpiece.

CHAPTER 11

Making Table Saw Jigs

A table saw jig holds the workpiece and guides it past the saw blade, so that it can be cut in some particular way. The five fundamental requirements of a good jig are:

1. It has to be accurately made.

2. It must not deflect or shift under the stress of sawing.

3. It should be guided by the saw's existing fence or table slots.

4. The workpiece must fasten securely to it.

5. The setup must be guarded so it does not expose the saw blade.

While many jigs accept workpieces within a size range, you should not also require them to be infinitely adjustable. Adjustability will compromise the fundamentals in search of a dubious usefulness that never quite happens. Universal jigs also tend to be large and unwieldy. It is better to tailor a new jig to each new situation, which adds the sixth requirement:

6. The jig must be easy, cheap and straightforward to make.

Three kinds of jig

Three basic kinds of jigs are suitable for the table saw:

auxiliary fences,

sled jigs,

box jigs.

Auxiliary fences have been discussed in crosscutting (page 101). The finger joint jig is a good example (page 150).

Sled jigs, which are fence-guided, clamp the workpiece and carry it to the saw blade. They are quick to make, and they're safe, because there's plenty of room to get a good grip. Positioning clamps out of the blade's path is the main setup problem. The pattern jig is a good example of a sled jig (page 128).

Box jigs allow you to stand the workpiece on end so you can cut joints. The tenon jig is a good example of a box jig (page 139).

Tools for making jigs

The main tool for making table saw jigs is, of course, the table saw. With it you'll need:

measuring tools,

one and preferably two cordless drills,

hammer and small nails,

clamps,

glue roller.

Fit one drill with a countersink-and-pilot hole bit, and the other with a screwdriver. An air-driven nailer or staple gun is a most useful investment now filtering down from professional shops into amateur hands.

There's no single best way to make jigs. This chapter contains good techniques, but jig design offers rich opportunities for your own cleverness. The more you understand about your equipment, the more success you'll have building and improving jigs.

Materials for making jigs

The fundamental requirement for jig-making material is stability. You want something that comes flat from the store and stays flat when you cut it and join it. There are two good, readily available solutions:

medium-density fiberboard (MDF);

particle board.

These sheet materials have dense surface layers and a softer interior, which makes them different from solid wood in that they cannot be joined by driving screws into an edge. The solution is to glue and screw wooden blocks to both mating faces. The result is an extremely strong and accurate joints. If you have an air compressor you can skip the screws, and simply glue and staple the parts together.

You might think plywood should be on this list. It isn't because it tends to twist. Use plywood for small parts like buttresses. Unlike MDF, you can screw directly into the edge of plywood.

Six-inch strips of MDF are about right for jig bases and faces, and 3/4 inch square clear softwood or poplar about right for glue blocks. It's very helpful to have a stock of both on hand.

Additional jig-making materials include:

plywood for buttresses, cabinet-grade maple or birch;

high density fiberboard (Masonite), for making templates and thin base plates;

yellow glue;

screws in various lengths;

toggle clamps.

With this kit of materials, you can make excellent jigs that will solve most table saw problems.

Jig-making techniques

Jigs hold the workpiece securely and in exactly the right orientation, while allowing you to move it to the saw blade. As you'll see in the example jigs, there are three essential jig-making techniques:

locating fences and stop blocks in the right place,

driving screws into MDF and particle board,

squarely joining fences and base plates.

Locating fences and stop blocks

Stop blocks position the workpiece on jigs. Make stop blocks out of 3/4-inch square lengths of softwood or poplar. In most situations a couple of No. 6 screws or several small nails are all you need to fasten a stop block to a jig base or fence. When you know the jig is permanent, roll glue onto block before assembly. Otherwise, leave it without glue so you can reposition the parts.

To accurately position a stop block, clamp the workpiece or a temporary fence in exactly the right place, then clamp the stop block to it. Now drill pilot holes to screw the stop block down tight.

Driving screws into jig parts

MDF and particle board tend to bulge upward when screws enter. The remedy is always to drill pilot holes, and to take the additional step of countersinking the pilot hole in the face of the sheet material.

Position the workpiece on the jig sled, then screw the stop block up tight against it.

Countersink pilot holes in MDF, so the material doesn't bulge upward.

Squarely joining jig parts

The basic method of joining MDF or particle board jig parts is to glue and screw a glue-block or buttress to one part, then glue and screw the other part to the block. For accuracy, always make the joint in two stages, not in a single glue-up. Plywood buttresses can be screwed directly to MDF jig bases, but for absolute accuracy add a glue block to them as well. Follow these steps:

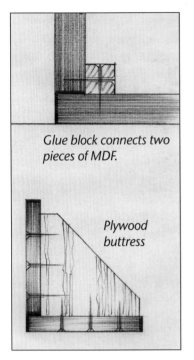

Glue block connects two pieces of MDF.

Plywood buttress

1. Position the glue block along one edge of the first jig part and draw a layout line. If you offset the pieces by 1/16 inch, you'll create a chip-clearance rebate.

2. Drill countersunk clearance holes through the glue block, with pilot holes into the MDF. Countersink the pilot holes in the MDF, to keep the material from bulging upward when you drive the screws.

4. Roll a thin layer of glue onto the wooden block. Use a small trim roller.

5. Reposition the block and drive the screws down tight.

6. Trim the combined edge of block and MDF on the table saw. The block now becomes a flange with a broad, flat base and parallel edges.

Glue-block flanges screwed to MDF plates make accurate jig parts.

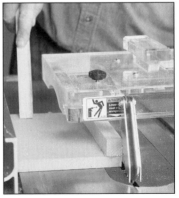

Trim the flange *and jig part together, to create a square and parallel surface.*

7. Clamp the assembly together to make layout lines, then drill countersunk clearance holes as needed to join the second piece of MDF to the glue block.

8. In many situations screws are enough to connect the second piece of MDF; keep them out of the saw bladeís path. For a permanent assembly, roll a thin layer of glue onto one of the mating surfaces.

9. Clamp the parts together and drive the first screw.

10. Check the alignment, then drive the remaining screws.

This basic jig joint can be used to make right-angled assemblies, as well as T-shaped sections. This building block solves many jig-making problems.

To make a glue block
flush and square, saw
a whisker off both
parts.

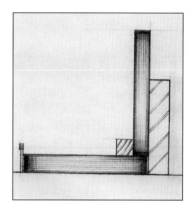

Saw a parallel edge
on the assembled
sled-and-fence.

Spreading Glue

The best tool for spreading glue is a small, disposable paint roller. Squeeze enough glue for the job at hand into the plastic tray that comes with the roller. Load the roller as you would with paint, but lightly. When you're done gluing, seal the roller and its tray into a zip-lock freezer bag. Glue doesn't get hard in the bottle and it won't get hard inside the bag. You'll be able to use the same two-bit roller for years if you want.

Pattern sawing jig

You can saw multiples of any straight-sided shape using a sled jig with fences to trap the work. Start with rectangular pieces of wood, located with stop blocks on two adjacent sides. For complex shapes, reposition the stop blocks for each successive cut, or lay them out sequentially on the sled. The pattern sawing jig is a good way to make buttresses for the 45-degree jig and panel-raising jig.

Pattern-sawing jig is an MDF sled with stop blocks to trap the workpiece. This jig cuts square blanks into precise 45-degree buttresses.

Air nailer *makes short work of attaching stop blocks to jig base.*

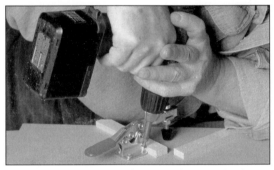

Lock the workpiece *in the jig with a toggle clamp screwed to the jig base.*

Guide the jig *along the saw fence to cut a buttress off the blank. In this situation the regular saw guard covers the blade.*

Pattern-sawing the accurate bird house

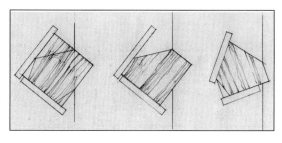

1. *Start with a rectangular workpiece. Draw the shape to be cut. Fit stop blocks to the jig sled and make the first cut.*
2. *Flip the workpiece over to make the second cut.*
3. *Reposition the stop blocks to make the last two cuts.*

Guards for shop-made jigs

Use the regular saw guard when you can, and devise a shop-made guard when the regular one won't work. Standard saw guards often contain recyclable parts.

Guard the blade from the top and sides. You may need to separate the top guard from the side guards, so the top guard can remain fixed while the side guards ride up and down.

Make see-through guards from shatterproof Lexan. You can cut, drill and smooth Lexan with ordinary woodworking tools. It glues to itself with an acetone-based solvent.

Make blade tunnels so the blade isn't exposed as it leaves the jig.

Limit the amount of guarding you must do by adding stop blocks to control the distance a jig can travel.

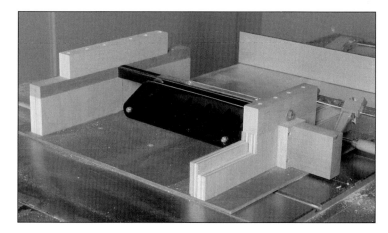

Crosscut box features a recycled blade guard, with a blade tunnel on the operator side.

Taper jig

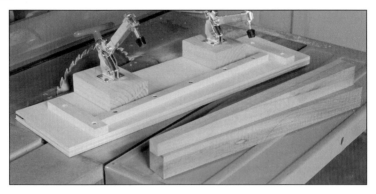

The taper jig saws wedges and tapered legs for furniture. You can taper two adjacent faces with a single jig set-up. When you want to taper all four faces, you'll need to move the jig fence, or make a second jig. Taper-cutting is not an everyday task, and this jig is so simple that it takes no time to unscrew and relocate the fence and stop blocks, or to make a new version, for each new taper.

1. Make the sled from plywood, MDF or particle board. The jig shown here has a 24-inch by 6 inch sled.

2. Mark the taper you want on the workpiece, then clamp it onto the sled with the excess wood hanging over the edge.

3. Drill and countersink clearance holes along the fence. Use the workpiece to position the fence, then screw it onto the sled.

4. Screw the stop blocks to the sled, tight to the ends of the workpiece.

5. Mount the toggle clamps so they hold the workpiece down tight. Be sure they're inboard of blade, guard and fence.

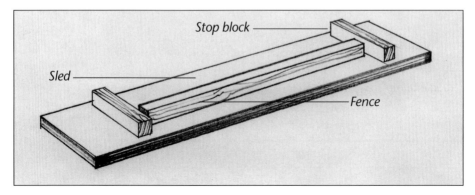

Stop block

Sled

Fence

Fit the stop blocks tight against the workpiece and screw them to the sled.

Lay out the taper on the leg blank and clamp it on the jig sled.

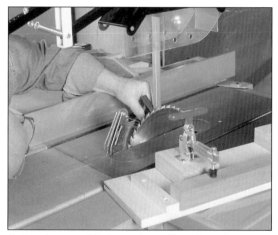

Mount the toggle clamps on the 2x4 blocks and adjust them to press tight on the workpiece.

Raise the saw blade so the gullets clear the top of the workpiece.

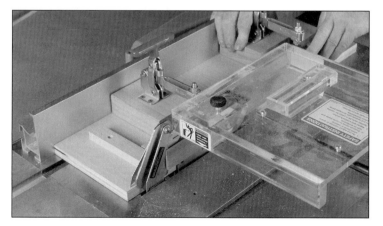

The taper jig in action. The toggle clamp mounting blocks are 1/8 inch away from the fence.

45-degree bevel jig

By making a 45-degree bevel on the edge or end of the workpiece, you can join the parts with a miter, which makes a seamless connection. This jig can also saw a spline slot into the face of the miter.

1. Cut the 20-inch by 6-inch sled and fence from 5/8 inch or 3/4-inch MDF. These dimensions will handle parts from 16 to 24 inches long.

2. Use the pattern-sawing jig to make three identical 45-degree buttresses from 3/4-inch plywood.

3. Square layout lines across the sled where the buttresses will go. Put the end buttresses several inches in from the ends of the sled and fence, to leave room for clamps. Drill clearance holes through the sled on the layout lines, countersunk both sides.

4. Roll glue onto the bottom face of one buttress, clamp it to the sled with the angled corner flush against the edge fence, and screw it in place. Glue, clamp and screw the remaining buttresses in the same way. If you prefer, clamp the jig fence to the edge of the sled, to help align the buttresses.

5. Position the jig fence on the angled edges of the plywood buttresses, using the saw table as a surface plate. Draw layout lines, drill clearance holes, roll glue, and screw the fence in its final position.

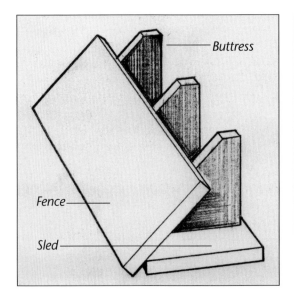

Buttress

Fence

Sled

The 45-degree bevel jig saws a 45-degree angle in the edges of the workpiece.

6. For sawing bevels on the ends of the workpiece, screw a stop to the jig fence. If you make the stop at least an inch square in section, you'll be able to clamp the workpiece to it.

It's not unusual to have to adjust a miter to 44 or 46 degrees, nor is it unusual to have a jig that's meant to saw 45 degrees come out a little bit off. To adjust the jig minutely, run strips of masking tape along the fence. Tape along the top edge of the fence decreases the miter angle. Tape along the bottom edge increases it.

This jig saws an excellent spline miter joint. To saw the spline slot in the miter, just turn the workpiece over in the jig and lower the blade, as discussed on page 147.

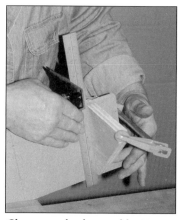

Clamp each plywood buttress to the jig base. Make it square and flush.

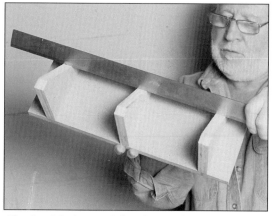

Check with the straightedge and tap the angled faces of the buttresses into alignment.

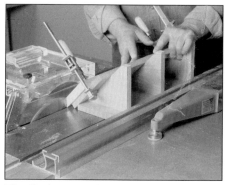

The jig in use. Rehearse its path with the saw turned off to make sure the work-holding clamps don't meet the blade or hang up on the guard.

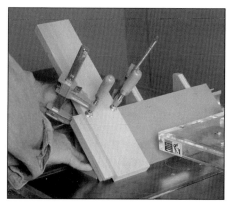

To saw a bevel on the end of the workpiece, screw a stop block to the jig fence.

Panel-raising jig

This useful jig holds a flat panel of wood up on edge so you can saw beveled edges and raised panels. It's made in the same way as the 45-degree bevel jig (page 132). The 20-inch jig shown here will handle panels ranging from 16 inches to 24 inches long; for other sizes, make a jig to suit.

To make the three buttresses, draw a cross-section of the panel you want and measure the angle, 10 degrees in this example. Use the sliding bevel to transfer the angle from the drawing to the pattern jig base.

When you load the jig, let the bottom edge of the panel rest on the saw table. Clamp the panel to the jig, and guide it with the saw fence. Saw the boundaries of the panel's center field with the wood flat on the saw table. It doesn't matter which you saw first, the center field or the beveled edge.

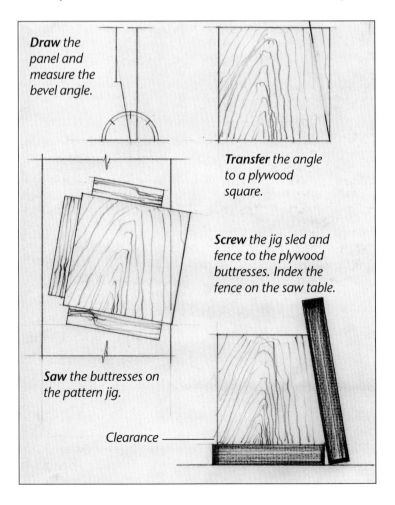

Draw the panel and measure the bevel angle.

Transfer the angle to a plywood square.

Screw the jig sled and fence to the plywood buttresses. Index the fence on the saw table.

Saw the buttresses on the pattern jig.

Clearance ⎯

***Panel-raising jig** allows you to make a raised panel entirely on the table saw.*

Clamp the panel to the face of the jig and saw the beveled edges. Move the saw fence to control the thickness of the bevel.

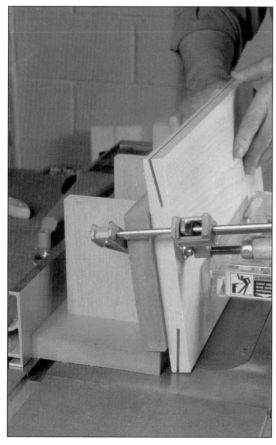

Saw the center field of the panel.

Crosscut box

The crosscut box is an important table saw jig. It is more accurate than the miter gauge, because it's guided by both table slots, and because it eliminates friction between the workpiece and saw table. Clamp stop blocks to the box wherever you need them, and add angled fences for sawing miters on the ends of frame pieces.

The box is not quick to make but it doesn't wear out, so it's worth making a nice one. However, it's not worth trying to make one size do every job. The one shown here is big enough for furniture parts. It's not uncommon to find several different sizes of crosscut box in a workshop.

The box rides on runners in both table slots. While you can make wooden runners to fit, mail-order suppliers now offer correctly sized bars with pre-drilled and tapped mounting holes.

The two bridge pieces hold the box together after its first use saws it in half. Make them out of hardwood.

The guard on the box shown here was cannibalized from a standard saw guard. The height of the fence and back board depend on the dimensions of this guard. If you don't have any guard parts to recycle, try making a top guard from a 6-inch wide plate of acrylic plastic. Add blade tunnels to guard the blade as it enters and leaves the box.

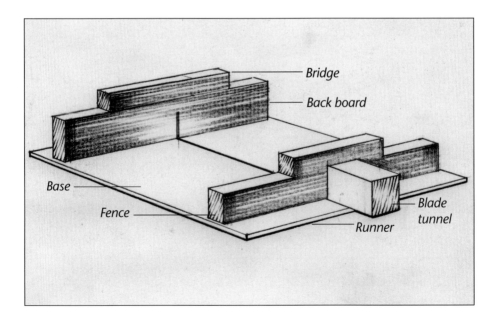

To build the crosscut box, follow these steps:

1. Cut the base from 1/4-inch tempered Masonite. The one shown measures 20 inches by 27 inches, same as the saw table.

2. Draw two parallel lines on the jig base, separated by the exact center-to-center distance between table slots. On the saw shown, this distance is 10-3/4 inches.

3. Set the runners on the parallel lines, and transfer the centers of the drilled holes to the jig base. Drill and countersink these holes in the jig base.

4. Drop the runners into the table slots and set the jig base on top. Line up the holes, then screw the jig base to the runners. Work the base back and forth, and adjust the tightness of the screws, until it slides easily and freely in the table slots.

5. Make the fence. The one shown is sawn from two thicknesses of plywood glued together, with a small chip-clearance rebate on the inside bottom edge. The high center accommodates the guard, while the stepped sides make it easy to hold and clamp the workpiece down low.

6. Fasten the fence to the jig base with a single screw at each end. This allows you to adjust it to dead square, and add more screws, after you saw the box (step 11).

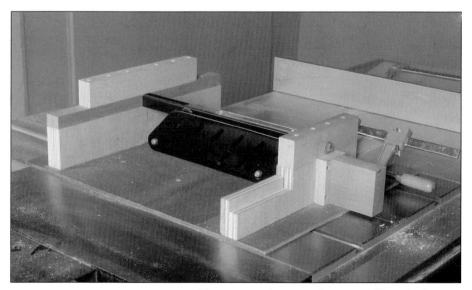

The crosscut box travels on metal bars in the table slots. The clamp holds a stop block.

7. Make the back board and screw it to the jig base. Since it won't need further adjustment, you can screw it down tight now. Add spacers as necessary to accommodate the blade guard.

8. Screw the bridge pieces to the fence and back board.

9. Screw the blade tunnels to the outside of the box, fore and aft.

10. Mount the box on the saw table, raise the saw blade, and push it smoothly through.

11. Turn off the saw and adjust the jig fence square to the new saw cut. Screw the fence down tight.

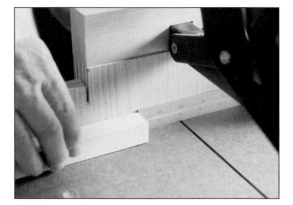

Locate a stop block in the crosscut box by measuring from the saw kerf. Clamp the block to the fence.

The crosscut box set up, with the workpiece clamped to the fence.

The crosscut box makes a perfectly square end on a long piece of wood.

Tenoning jig

The tenoning jig makes tenons and open mortises on the ends of rails and stiles. You can make both parts of the open mortise-and-tenon joint with this jig and they can come straight from the saw. This design has plenty of accessible clamping surfaces for holding the workpiece in place; there's more on using the jig on page 154.

The tenoning jig is a box jig that relies on the technique of gluing and screwing blocks to pieces of medium-density fiberboard (MDF), as detailed on page 126. Use 1-1/4 inch screws with 5/8-inch or 3/4-inch MDF and 3/4-inch by 3/4-inch glue blocks. When you assemble the jig, do it on the saw table, because that's likely the flattest surface in the shop.

Tenoning jig, which moves along the saw fence, has blade tunnels fore and aft.

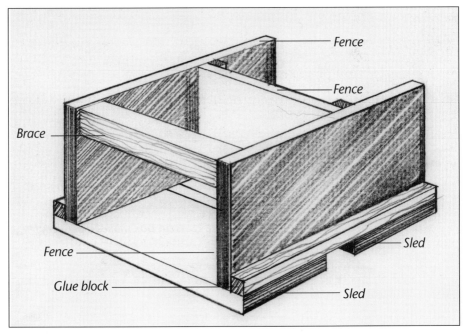

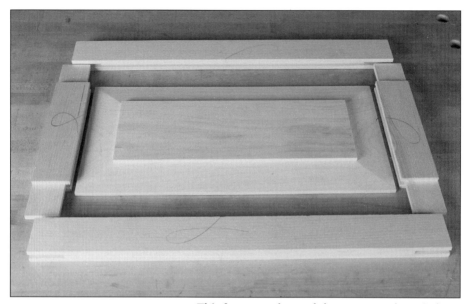

This frame-and-panel door was made entirely on the table saw, using the tenoning jig and the panel-raising jig.

CHAPTER 12

Sawing Joints

Joining wood is a complex subject and there are hundreds of joint variations. The good news is that once you have an accurate table saw, you have good solutions for a wide variety of joining problems.

From the point of view of the wood, there are three broad categories of joints:

Long-grain joints. The grain of both pieces runs the same direction. Edge-to-edge, this joint makes wide panels and tops out of narrow boards. The right-angle form makes legs and columns. The face to face form makes structural beams.

Rail joints. The end-grain of one stick of wood joins into the side grain of another stick. These joints make frames, leg-and-rail assemblies for tables and chairs, beds, and doors.

Case joints. Two wide panels of wood meet at a corner, making boxes, drawers, and carcases. All joints in plywood, particle board, and MDF are case joints.

From the perspective of joint structure, there are three basic kinds of joints, all held together with glue. They are:

Two-part joints, primarily edge-to-edge butt joints and right-angle butts, and long-grain miters. These joints, which come straight from the saw, hold together with glue alone.

Two-part interlocking joints, such as the mortise-and-tenon, bridle, dovetail, and finger joints. Tenons, bridles and finger-type joints can come straight from the saw, but mortises and dovetails need additional tools.

Three-part joints, where a third piece of wood makes the bridge between the two primary elements. This group includes splines, which come off the saw, plus dowels, loose tenons and biscuit joints, which do not.

All table saw joints have one thing in common. Neatly fitting parts can only come from accurately dimensioned stock. This is because the ends of each piece of wood register on the fence or stop block. This means that the between-shoulders distance, the critical dimension in furniture making, springs from the finished length of the workpiece.

Even a well-made joint will glue up badly if it's not correctly clamped. With each joint in this section, I've also included the clamping procedure.

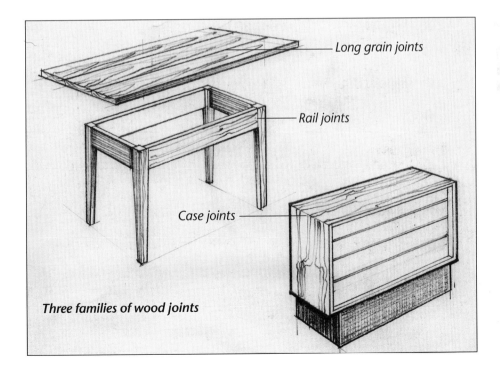

Long grain joints

Rail joints

Case joints

Three families of wood joints

Butt joints

You can make a long-grain butt joint directly from the table saw. A carbide-tipped blade creates a flat and square edge that is smooth enough for gluing. This is the simplest directly glued two-part joint.

The long-grain butt joint makes two different shapes: flat and right-angled. The flat edge-to-edge butt joint allows you to combine any number of narrow boards into a wide panel. The right-angled butt joint makes a strong structural element for legs, columns, boxes, and frames.

Making a long-grain butt joint directly from the saw is a ripping operation. Square the blade to the table and set the fence short, as discussed on page 79. Then follow these steps:

1. Assemble the boards in the order you like, and mark each joint so you can get them back together.

2. Crosscut all the wood to finished length plus 1 inch.

3. Choose and mark the straightest edge on each piece of wood. Run this edge against the fence and saw the other edge straight and parallel. Now rotate the wood end for end and saw the first edge off it. Make each rip cut in a single motion, without hesitation. If you pause during the cut, you will not end up with the smoothest edge.

4. Set up each joint on edge. Make sure each joint is flat and tight, and if it isn't, either saw the wood again or get out your hand tools and plane it.

Assemble the butt joint in bar clamps. A hammer, with a protective block, taps the boards into line with one another.

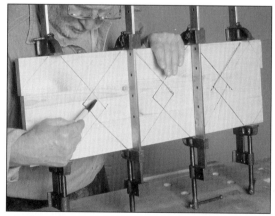

Marker triangles show how the pressure from each clamp fans out at 45 degrees, covering the whole glue line. Imagining these fans helps you figure out how many clamps the glueup needs.

5. Roll glue onto both surfaces of each joint and assemble all the parts in bar clamps. Keep the pieces flat by alternating clamps top and bottom and make them finger-tight.

6. Put C-clamps and blocks across each joint to bring the wood surfaces into line. Push each joint flat and smooth, while you tighten the bar clamps.

The difficult part of this joint is keeping the boards aligned. Before you blame the saw, check and see whether the wood isn't distorted. A small amount of twist or bow can throw the whole panel off. One solution is to add a spline (page 145).

Right-angle butt joint

Prepare the wood for the right-angle butt joint exactly the same as for the flat panel. Put the two pieces together dry to make a layout line, then roll glue onto both mating surfaces. Set up the joint in bar clamps, or with C-clamps. Use clamping blocks to help retain squareness.

To make a leg, pedestal, or column, join two right angles, then glue them together. A square column can be made in two different ways. One way requires starting with two different widths of wood. The other method uses four pieces all the same size, arranged pinwheel fashion. .

When you use the right-angled joint to connect two pieces of plywood or MDF, add glue blocks inside the corner.

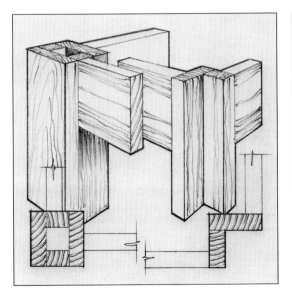

C-clamps hold the long-grain right angle together. To make a column or a box, first make two long right angles.

Tongue and groove corner joint

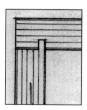

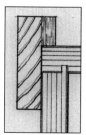

The tongue-and-groove corner joint makes a sturdy box or drawer straight from the saw. Both parts of the joint can be made with a regular saw blade and fence. It doesn't require any jigs or special cutters. The joint is equally useful in solid wood or in plywood and other sheet materials.

Locate and dimension the tongue as shown in the drawing. The joint always involves short grain, which is weak. That's why a large tongue doesn't strengthen the joint, it weakens it. Similarly, trying to center the tongue also weakens the joint. The joint will be plenty strong with a tongue that's 1/8 inch thick and up to 1/4 inch long, depending on the thickness of the wood.

1. Cut all the wood parts to finished size.

2. With the end of the wood bearing against the saw fence, saw the grooves. Make the groove depth a hair greater than the tongue length, so the shoulders pull up tight.

3. Now make the tongue pieces. With the end of the work bearing on the fence, raise the saw blade to just shy of the final thickness of the tongue and saw the shoulder.

4. Stand the workpiece up on end against the fence to saw the face of the tongue. Saw with the tongue away from the fence, so any error leaves the tongue too thick, and correctable, rather than too thin, and ruined.

5. Clamp the joint with glue blocks as shown, in order to put pressure over the joint itself. Inboard squeeze would bow the wood, opening the joint.

Clamping block puts squeeze over joint.

Saw the grooves first. *Then saw the tongues.*

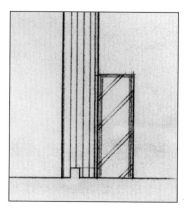

Saw with the tongue *away from the fence.*

Long-grain spline joint

A spline is a thin piece of wood let into grooves in both mating pieces of wood. It is the simplest kind of three-part joint. While the spline does increase the strength of the joint, its main purpose is aligning the surfaces. However, the spline will not help you align badly distorted wood, because you can't saw accurate grooves in the first place.

Usually it is simplest to make the spline out of the same wood you're joining together, with the grain running the same direction. A cross-grain spline is not necessary for strength, and it's almost impossible to saw and assemble accurately. Similarly, don't make plywood splines. They're likely to come apart under load.

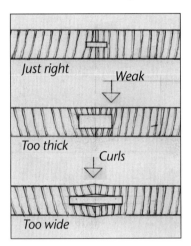

Just right
Weak

Too thick
Curls

Too wide

Make the spline a comfortable fit in the thickness of the saw kerf. A thick spline weakens the final joint, with failure likely at the root of the spline. In width, anything up to 3/4 inch will not cause problems, but extra-wide splines invite the wood to curl, opening the joint.

Center the groove for the spline by eye in the thickness of the wood. A small distance off-center doesn't matter, as long as you run the face side of each piece against the saw fence. The depth of the groove should be half the width of the spline, plus 1/64 inch.

To assemble the joint, roll a thin coat of glue on the spline, and brush a little glue inside the groove, just enough to dampen the wood. Too much glue is counterproductive. It will act as a hydraulic ram when you clamp the joint, forcing the wood to curl away from the spline.

Rip thin splines off the edge of a wider board. Set the blade low and use a push stick.

Long-grain miter joint

A long-grain miter can make a leg or a pedestal that looks as if it was made from a large chunk of solid wood. This two-part glue joint gives you a lot of design freedom.

Saw the wood using the 45-degree bevel jig (page 00). For repeatable accuracy, size the jig to the job at hand. Saw all the wood to finished width, with truly parallel edges, before mitering.

Register the corner of the wood on the saw table and clamp it to the jig. Make sure the wood is tight against the jig by clamping as low down as you can without tangling the clamp into the saw blade. Raise the saw blade so it just breaks the top surface of the workpiece, and bring the saw guard as close to the top of the cut as you can.

When there are a lot of pieces to be sawn to the same size, make the jig large enough for an end stop block. Clamp the first workpiece to the jig, then use it to align the stop block.

Clamping this joint is not easy and there aren't any short-cuts. You have to get pressure across the joint lines. There are two ways. One way is to use removable masking tape, which is blue, instead of clamps. Lay the mitered pieces flat on the bench, with the points of the miters just touching one another, and tape across them. Then flip the assembly over, roll glue onto the faces of the miters, and fold the pieces together. Tighten the clamping action by stretching more masking tape across the joints.

The second way to glue up this joint is by gluing 45-degree clamping blocks on the outside of all the miters. This gives you positive control of clamping pressure directly across the glue line. When the glue sets, saw the clamping blocks off the workpiece and clean up by planing or sanding.

Long-grain miter has plenty of glue surface so it is strong. Temporarily glued clamping blocks ensure a tight joint.

Register the corner of the wood on the saw table and clamp it to the 45-degree jig. Before you saw, adjust for clearance between clamps, saw guard and splitter (below).

Tape the four mitered pieces together and roll glue into the joints.

Fold up the column and press the joints together.

Stretch tape tightly across the last joint. Any error in sawing the miters will show up here.

End miter and spline miter

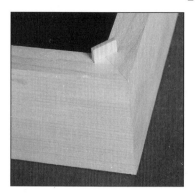

Saw the end miter in the same way as the long-grain miter. Attach a right-angle fence to the face of the jig, as shown in the photo, to position the workpiece.

A spline both locates the parts and strengthens the miter joint. However, if it's not to weaken the joint, the spline should be located right at the root of the miter, as shown in the drawing. Make the spline a push fit in the saw kerf, and don't worry about it being cross-grain.

Use the 45-degree bevel jig to saw the spline slots. Load the workpiece onto the jig so the face of the miter is tight against the saw table. Clamp it low down on the jig.

The best way to glue up this joint is first to glue temporary clamping blocks onto the wood, as discussed on page 146. As an alternative, the splined miter can be directly clamped with tape. Fit all four pieces together and close them partway with hand pressure. Then tape across the joint lines and pull hard to close them.

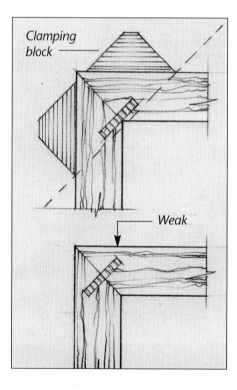

Clamping block

Weak

Locate the spline at the root of the miter. Shifting the spline outward weakens the joint at the arrow. Dotted line shows length of clamping blocks. Keep them off the outside corner so you can see the joint close.

Use a narrow push stick to rip some width off a spline.

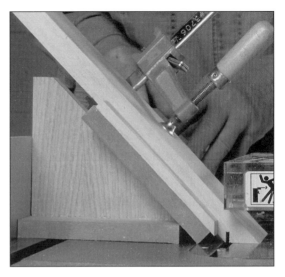

To cut an end miter, *screw a stop to the 45-degree jig*

Turn the workpiece *over to saw the spline slot. For maximum strength, saw the slot right at the root of the miter.*

Face frame mitered and splined

You can make the miter in the width of the wood instead of in its thickness. This joint has no strength when directly glued, but inserting and gluing a spline makes a strong corner. It's especially useful for face frames on cabinets.

Saw the slot *for the spline using a 45-degree backup block.*

Gluing the spline *makes a strong corner joint.*

Finger joint

The finger joint, also known as the box joint or comb joint, makes a strong and attractive box or drawer in solid wood or plywood. Its straight lines enhance the architecture of the corner, especially in uniform laminate birch plywood.

It is a two-part glued joint that comes straight off the table saw. There is no limit to the size of pieces it can join. The width of the blade determines the joint spacing, so use cutters from a dado head to get the finger width you want. Make a sample joint to adjust the setup, then when it's right, saw all the wood.

To assemble the joint, brush glue onto all the mating surfaces, and pull the joints home with clamps. Then set a clamp across each joint until the glue dries.

Make a fence of 3/4-inch wood measuring 18 inches long and about 2 1/2 inches wide. Mount the dado head and raise it to the thickness of the workpiece, minus 1/32 inch. Hold the fence on the miter gauge and saw through it.

Drill and countersink pilot holes, and screw the 2-inch wide Masonite base to the auxiliary fence, with no screw in the saw's way.

Make a locating key the exact size of the kerf in the fence. Make it about 8 inches long, then saw off a 2-inch piece. Fit the short piece into the kerf. Space the fence along the miter gauge with the 6-inch length of locating key. Clamp and screw the fence to the gauge.

Raise the dado head to the exact thickness of the workpiece and saw a second kerf through the fence. Add a blade tunnel on the operator side. This completes the finger joint jig.

To make the finger joint, stand the first workpiece on end, tight to the fence key, and clamp it. Saw the first slot. Move the workpiece so the sawn slot fits over the fence key and saw again. For accuracy, clamp the wood in each position.

Use the long key to offset the second workpiece, then saw the first slot right at the edge of the wood. Fit the cutout over the fence key to saw the next slot. Make a test joint to check the fit and adjust the distance between the key and the blade until the joint faces are snug.

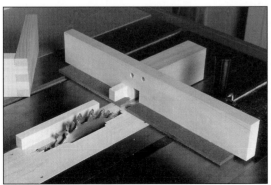

Adjust the fit of the test joint by tapping the jig right or left with a light hammer. Raise and lower the dado cutter for different thicknesses of wood. To change the width of the slots, make another jig.

Half lap

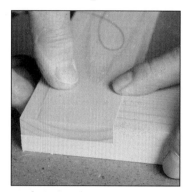

Both parts of the half-lap joint are the same.

With modern glue, the half-lap makes a serviceable corner joint. The shoulders make a positive stop in both directions. Though it's not particularly elegant, in very thin wood it might be the only corner joint you can make. It doesn't matter whether you saw the joint's shoulder or face first.

Saw the joint face using the tenoning jig. Adjust the setup by clamping a test piece to the jig fence, with its end down tight on the saw table. Raise the saw blade to cut the full depth in one pass. Move the saw fence so the blade cuts away exactly half the thickness of the wood. Start the cut, then withdraw it and check the dimension with your dial caliper. When you get it right, saw all the half-lap faces in the same way.

Saw the shoulder of the joint using the miter gauge or crosscut box. Raise the saw blade to cut dead on the finished dimension, so the ATB blade doesn't leave a score in the face of the workpiece.

To set up for sawing the face of the joint, raise the saw blade to the exact width of the wood.

To saw the face of the joint, clamp the workpiece in the tenoning jig.

Saw the joint shoulder on the miter gauge, using a stop block.

Cross lap

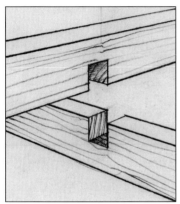

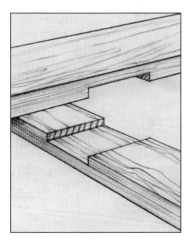

The cross lap or cross-halving is a useful joint for stands and table bases. Saw it on the miter gauge, using the dado head.

For accuracy, clean up the wood to finished thickness first. When the cross-lapped pieces fit together edge-to-edge, you'll be able to shim the dado head to this exact thickness. When they fit face-to-face, use stop blocks to locate the extremities and make multiple passes over the cutter.

The real problem is locating the cross lap in the exact center of the wood. One way is to start with extra-long wood. Saw the joint in about the center, then make a stop block that exactly fills the cutouts. Clamp the stop block to the miter gauge or crosscut box so you can saw both ends of each piece at the same setting.

A dado cutter makes the joint. Use a stop block and clamp the wood to the fence. Move the stop block to make the second cut, which opens the joint to its finished width.

Open mortise and tenon

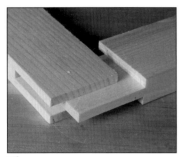

Of the many forms of the mortise and tenon joint, the open mortise, or bridle joint, is the only one that can be entirely made on the table saw. It requires the miter gauge or crosscut box, and the tenoning jig.

For maximum strength, lay out the joint so the thickness of the tenon is just less than the combined thickness of both mortise cheeks. Center the joint in the wood.

The open mortise and tenon is a sturdy joint that can come straight from the table saw.

There are two ways to make the mortise, using a dado head or using a flat-top saw blade. The dado head can cut the mortise in one pass, but only up to about 2 inches deep. The flat-top blade can go up to 3 inches, but it requires making multiple cuts. While you could saw the mortise with a regular ATB blade, you won't get a flat bottom.

To cut the mortise with a dado head, assemble the cutters to the exact thickness and clamp a test piece in the tenoning jig. Raise the cutter to final depth, then make the test cut. Measure the thickness of both mortise cheeks with the dial caliper. Adjust the fence until both cheeks are the same thickness, which means the mortise is on center. After sawing both cheeks on all the parts, move the fence to waste the center of the mortise.

When sawing the tenon, it doesn't matter which you cut first, the shoulder or the face. Cut the shoulders against a stop block on the miter gauge or in the crosscut box. Cut the faces in the tenoning jig. Cut one tenon face, then turn the wood around and cut the other at the same setting.

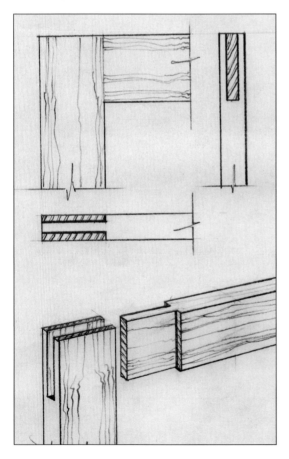

Cut both tenon cheeks at the same setting, using a flat-top saw blade. The blade tunnel, foreground, guards the blade before it enters the jig body.

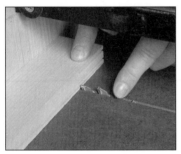

Saw the tenon shoulders with the crosscut box. Raise the blade to touch the inside corner, without sawing into the tenon face.

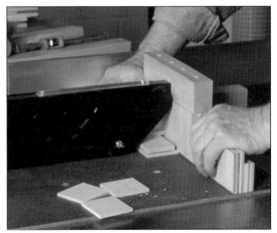

Set the dado cutter to the full depth of the mortise. Use a small square to set the distance from the cutter to the inside of the tenoning jig.

Torsion box

Like an airplane wing, the torsion box is made by sandwiching a grid of ribs called the core between two thin plywood skins. The torsion box exploits the best qualities of solid wood, plywood and glue, offering amazing strength and rigidity for minimum weight. Torsion boxes not only make excellent substrates for veneer, plastic laminate or leather, they also are versatile construction elements for all kinds of furniture. T-boxes can be made straight from the table saw.

The torsion box is an extremely strong and versatile furniture and building element that you can make straight from the table saw.

1. **Design the core.** It's a simple framework of wood stapled together. The staples aren't structural, they merely prevent the core from flopping around while you glue the skins. Tailor the core to include ledger pockets for joining a shelf to a wall or to other furniture elements. The thickness of core material can be anywhere from 1/4 inch to 3/4 inch. The skins usually are 1/4 inch thick. The width of the core stock, plus the thickness of the skins, is the finished thickness of the box. Keep the on-center spacing of core pieces no more than 12 times the skin thickness.

2. **Make the core.** Saw the core pieces to accurate length and width, with square ends. Staple the core pieces together one side at a time, using extra pieces of core material as spacer blocks.

3. **Make the skins.** You can use hardwood-faced plywood for a polished surface, or birch for a painted surface. Saw the top and bottom skins to finished length and width. Set the core in position on each skin and hot-glue small locating blocks onto the skins in each corner.

4. **Glue up the box.** Roll yellow glue onto one side of the core and fit it onto the skin. Roll glue on the other side of the core and add the second skin. Clamp the assembly atop the workbench, using wooden cauls, or trap it between two pieces of 3/4-inch particle board cut to the dimensions of the box..

5. **Complete the box** by gluing on a solid wood edge, then finish it by painting, varnishing, or covering with leather.

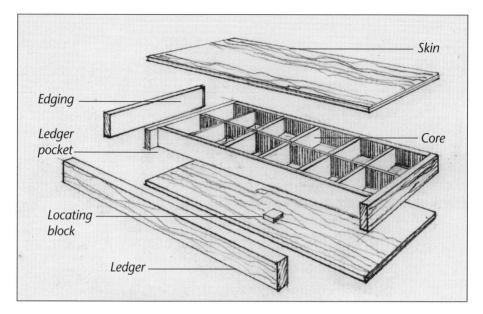

Skin

Edging

Ledger
pocket

Core

Locating
block

Ledger

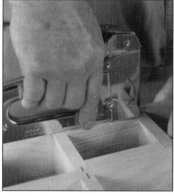

Staple the core pieces together, without glue. Staple both sides.

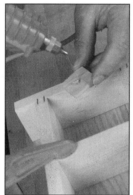

Hot-glue locating blocks onto the skins.

Roll glue onto the core and fit the skins.

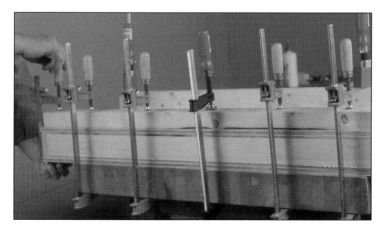

Glue up on a flat surface, with 2x4s as clamping cauls to distribute the squeeze.

Frame-and-panel

The frame and panel door can go together straight from the saw.

Put a rectangular frame together with a raised-and-fielded panel, and you've got a cabinet door, an element of traditional wall paneling, or the side of a bureau. A groove around the inside edge of the frame holds the panel in place; for a different look, you can trap the panel with a small molding instead. In solid wood, there has to be enough space between the panel and the bottom of the groove for the wood to move. Here is a way to make a frame and panel straight from the table saw:

1. Draw the frame and panel full size in cross section, so you know the detailed dimensions. Make the groove the same width as the open mortise (page 154), then make the panel thickness to fit it.

2. Saw the panel using the panel-raising jig (page 134).

3. Make the frame using open mortise and tenon joints. Make the joints a hair shy of being flush, so you can clamp the pieces in both directions. When you set the saw blade or dado head for the depth of the open mortise, subtract the depth of the groove.

4. Saw the panel-retaining groove centered on the inside edge of all four frame pieces. The groove will remove a piece from the tenons. But you compensated for that when you cut the mortise.

5. Assemble the frame around the panel. Glue the corner joints, but don't glue the panel in its groove.

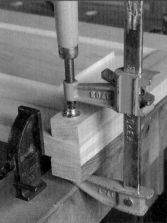

Clamp the frame both ways, so the joints seat tight. A clamp across the mortise cheeks ensures a closed joint and a good glue line.

Index

Index continued

Photographs:	John Kelsey
Drawings:	Ian Kirby
Design and layout:	Glee Barre
Photo scanning:	Morgan Kelsey
Griping:	Dag Nabbit
Paper:	Silverado Matte
Typeface:	Stone serif, sans and informal
Manufacturing:	Vaughan Printing, Nashville, TN USA